REGENTS RENAISSANCE DRAMA SERIES

General Editor: Cyrus Hoy
Advisory Editor: G. E. Bentley

THE JEW OF MALTA

CHRISTOPHER MARLOWE

The Jew of Malta

Edited by

RICHARD W. VAN FOSSEN

UNIVERSITY OF NEBRASKA PRESS · LINCOLN

Publishers on the Plains

MANUFACTURED IN THE UNITED STATES OF AMERICA

FOR ANN

This lady is no clog, as many are.

Regents Renaissance Drama Series

The purpose of the Regents Renaissance Drama Series is to provide soundly edited texts, in modern spelling, of the more significant plays of the Elizabethan, Jacobean, and Caroline theater. Each text in the series is based on a fresh collation of all sixteenth- and seventeenth-century editions. The textual notes, which appear above the line at the bottom of each page, record all substantive departures from the edition used as the copy-text. Variant substantive readings among sixteenth- and seventeenth-century editions are listed there as well. In cases where two or more of the old editions present widely divergent readings, a list of substantive variants in editions through the seventeenth century is given in an appendix. Editions after 1700 are referred to in the textual notes only when an emendation originating in some one of them is received into the text. Variants of accidentals (spelling, punctuation, capitalization) are not recorded in the notes. Contracted forms of characters' names are silently expanded in speech prefixes and stage directions, and, in the case of speech prefixes, are regularized. Additions to the stage directions of the copy-text are enclosed in brackets. Stage directions such as "within" or "aside" are enclosed in parentheses when they occur in the copy-text.

Spelling has been modernized along consciously conservative lines. "Murther" has become "murder," and "burthen," "burden," but within the limits of a modernized text, and with the following exceptions, the linguistic quality of the original has been carefully preserved. The variety of contracted forms (*'em*, *'am*, *'m*, *'um*, *'hem*) used in the drama of the period for the pronoun *them* are here regularly given as *'em*, and the alternation between *a'th'* and *o'th'* (for *on* or *of the*) is regularly reproduced as *o'th'*. The copy-text distinction between preterite endings in *-d* and *-ed* is preserved except where the elision of *e* occurs in the penultimate syllable; in such cases, the final syllable is contracted. Thus, where the old editions read "threat'ned," those of the present series read "threaten'd." Such contracted preterites in *-y'd* as "try'd," "cry'd," "deny'd," in the old editions, are here given as "tried," "cried," "denied."

Punctuation has been brought into accord with modern practices. The effort here has been to achieve a balance between the generally light pointing of the old editions, and a system of punctuation which, without overloading the text with exclamation marks, semicolons, and dashes, will make the often loosely flowing verse (and prose) of the original syntactically intelligible to the modern reader. Dashes are regularly used only to indicate interrupted speeches, or shifts of address within a single speech.

Explanatory notes, chiefly concerned with glossing obsolete words and phrases, are printed below the textual notes at the bottom of each page. References to stage directions in the notes follow the admirable system of the Revels editions, whereby stage directions are keyed, decimally, to the line of the text before or after which they occur. Thus, a note on 0.2 has reference to the second line of the stage direction at the beginning of the scene in question. A note on 115.1 has reference to the first line of the stage direction following line 115 of the text of the relevant scene.

CYRUS HOY

University of Rochester

Contents

Acknowledgments

Most of the work for this edition was done at the Folger Shakespeare Library, where I was fortunate enough to hold a fellowship during the summer of 1962. I am grateful to the Library not only for making my work possible but for the warm hospitality and delightful company which are uniquely the Folger's. Research for the edition was also aided by a grant from Cornell College.

I wish to thank the authorities of the Huntington Library, the Houghton Library, and the Library of Congress for providing me with Xerox prints of their copies of the 1633 quarto. My secretary, Patricia Romer, has provided careful assistance in proofreading.

R. W. V. F.

Cornell College
Mount Vernon, Iowa

List of Abbreviations
(Excluding editions, for which see pp. xxix–xxx)

conj.	conjecture
Cooper	Thomas Cooper. *Thesaurus Linguae Romanae & Britannicae.* London, 1584.
Deighton	Kenneth Deighton. *The Old Dramatists: Conjectural Readings on the Texts....* Westminster, 1896.
ELH	*ELH: A Journal of English Literary History*
Harvey	Sir Paul Harvey. *The Oxford Companion to Classical Literature.* Oxford, 1937.
Hurwitz	Solomon T. H. Hurwitz. "Jews and Jewesses in English Literature," *Jewish Forum*, V (June, 1922), 198–203.
imp.	imperfect
Koeppel	Emil Koeppel. "Zur Quellenkunde des Stuart-Dramas," *Archiv für das Studium der Neueren Sprachen und Litteraturen*, XCVII (1896), 323–329.
MLR	*Modern Language Review*
Nares	Robert Nares. *A Glossary....* London, 1822.
Onions	C. T. Onions. *A Shakespeare Glossary.* 2nd edn. Oxford, 1919.
OED	*Oxford English Dictionary*
RES	*Review of English Studies*
Seaton	Ethel Seaton. "Fresh Sources for Marlowe," *RES*, V (1929), 385–401.
S.D.	stage direction
S.P.	speech prefix
Spivack	Bernard Spivack. *Shakespeare and the Allegory of Evil.* New York, 1958.
STC	A. W. Pollard & G. R. Redgrave. *A Short-Title Catalogue of Books Printed in England...1475–1640.* London, 1926.
subs.	in substance
TLS	*The Times* (London) *Literary Supplement*

Introduction

One group of entries in the so-called *Diary* of Philip Henslowe, Elizabethan theater owner and theatrical manager, consists of a record of daily receipts (or Henslowe's portion thereof) "from performances at his theatres between 19 February 1591/2 and 5 November 1597."[1] In this list occurs the first known reference to Christopher Marlowe's remarkable drama, *The Jew of Malta*, apparently one of the most popular plays of its time. Since it was performed over a period of some five years by all of the companies associated with Henslowe (thirty-six times, in all), we may assume that the manager owned the rights to the play himself. The continued success of the play (and its receipts were considerably higher than Henslowe's average) may well have been stimulated by the sensation surrounding the arrest (January, 1594) and execution (June 7) of Dr. Lopez, Queen Elizabeth's physician, who was a Jew; at any rate, contemporaneously with this *cause célèbre* a ballad certainly capitalizing on Marlowe's play was entered on the Register of the Stationers Company, the copyright book of London publishers, by John Danter:

xvj ^{to} maij

John danter   Entred for his copie vnder th[e h]and of master warder **Cawood**/ a ballad intituled/ *the murtherous life and terrible death of the riche Jew of Malta*   vj^{d}C[2]

On the very next day, the play itself was registered for publication:

xvij ^{to} maij

Nicholas Linge   Entred for theire copie vnder the hand
Thomas Mill-   of Master Warder **Cawood** *the famouse*
ington   *tragedie of the Riche Jewe of Malta*   vj^{d}C[3]

[1] R. A. Foakes and R. T. Rickert, eds., *Henslowe's Diary* (Cambridge, 1961), p. xxiv.

[2] Edward Arber, ed., *A Transcript of the Registers of the Company of Stationers of London: 1554–1640 A.D.* (London, 1875–1894), II, 649.

[3] Arber, II, 650.

No copy of either of these items has survived—if, indeed, they were printed. Hence it is that we must rely for our text of *The Jew of Malta* on a quarto of 1633, registered as follows:

20º Nouembris 1632

Nicholas vavasor   Entred for his Copy vnder the handes of Sir HENRY HERBERT and Master **Weaver** warden a Tragedy called *the Jew of Malta*. [by Christopher Marlowe]   vj[d4]

But the play by no means disappeared from sight during the intervening years. In 1598, Henslowe took an inventory of costumes and properties belonging to the Lord Admiral's men; among the articles in this fascinating list is "j cauderm for the Jewe."[5] The play was apparently refurbished in 1601, when two further entries appear in the *Diary*:

Lent vnto Robart shawe & m^r Jube the 19 of maye 1601 to bye divers thinges for the Jewe of malta the some of   v[ll]

lent mor to the littell tayller the same daye for more thinges for the Jewe of malta some of   xs[6]

It is even likely that Marlowe's work was performed on the Continent by English actors: there are records of a play *"von dem Juden"* at Passau in 1607 and Gräz in 1608, and a *Tragödie von Barabas, Juden von Malta*, at Dresden in 1626.[7]

When revived in England in 1632 by Queen Henrietta's company, the play was staged at the Cock-pit (or Phoenix) theater and at the court, with the prologues and epilogues written for these occasions by Thomas Heywood and included in this edition. Allusions in seventeenth-century sources attest to the play's continued reputation,

4 Arber, IV, 288.

5 Foakes and Rickert, p. 321. The "cauderm," of course, is the caldron employed in the last scene of the play.

6 Foakes and Rickert, p. 170.

7 E. K. Chambers, *The Elizabethan Stage* (Oxford, 1923), III, 425; II, 281; II, 285–286.

and it appears to have remained available in printed form as late as 1671.[8]

The date when Marlowe wrote *The Jew of Malta*—like the problem of its sources and, indeed, the question of its authorship in its present state—remains uncertain. If we assume that the prologue spoken by Machiavelli was written at the same time as the play proper, the death of the third Duke of Guise (referred to in l. 3), December 23, 1588, provides a *terminus a quo*; the first entry in Henslowe, February 26, 1592, makes a firm *terminus ad quem*. Within the span of time thus defined, critics tend to place the play early or late depending upon their feelings about its stylistic and structural maturity; but the folly of such a procedure is obvious if one thinks of the anomalies in the development of a Tennessee Williams or a William Faulkner. Short of the unlikely eventuality that convincing contemporary documentation turns up, it is surely best to agree with Tucker Brooke that "the year 1590 cannot be far wrong."[9]

For a number of reasons, the prevailing tendency in Marlowe scholarship has been to argue that the play in the form we know it has been heavily revised on one or more occasions, possibly by Thomas Heywood: (1) more than forty years intervened between the writing of the play and the printing of the version that has come down to us; (2) an old-fashioned play would presumably have had to be "brought up to date" for production at the fashionable court of King Charles I and Queen Henrietta Maria; (3) the text of the 1633 quarto is seriously corrupt; (4) the manner and quality of the play deteriorate badly in the third and fourth acts; (5) Marlowe was incapable of producing the comedy that pervades so many scenes. In recent years, however, it has become more and more common to defend the 1633 text as very probably a faithful version of what Marlowe wrote. The validity of this approach will be supported on critical grounds in this introduction and on textual grounds in the "Note on the Text."

No source is known for Marlowe's story, but a variety of origins has been suggested for various elements in the play. The historical

---

[8] F. S. Boas, *Christopher Marlowe: A Biographical and Critical Study* (Oxford, 1940), pp. 297–299, and [C. F.] Tucker Brooke, "The Reputation of Christopher Marlowe," *Transactions of the Connecticut Academy of Arts and Sciences*, XXV (June, 1922), 379–382.

[9] C. F. Tucker Brooke, ed., *The Works of Christopher Marlowe* (Oxford, 1910), p. 230.

framework—most unhistorical in Marlowe's handling—is provided by the famous Turkish attack on Malta in 1565. The character of Barabas may have been suggested by the career of either or both of two sixteenth-century Jews, Juan Miques and David Passi.[10] The trick employed by Barabas and Ithamore on Friar Jacomo is derived from a story long popular in many forms; the fact that the subplot of Heywood's *The Captives* is a fuller version of the same anecdote, indeed, has been regarded—without sufficient warrant—as evidence for Heywood's hand in *The Jew of Malta*.[11] Bakeless suggests many other possible specific sources, most of them demanding a considerable reliance on hypothesis.[12] One last source is quite clear: the Bible. In the explanatory notes to the play, attention is called to the many names derived from Old Testament sources, to Barabas' frequent use of Old Testament passages in allusion, paraphrase, and even quotation, and to New Testament doctrines referred to by the Christians and by Barabas—doctrines that the Christians characteristically pervert or, at best, fail to live up to.

Apart from these specific sources, two rather more general influences contribute a great deal to the effect of the play as a whole; these are the conceptions, or misconceptions, of Jewish character and of Machiavellian doctrine that might almost be said to underlie everything else.

First it must be realized that the portrait of Barabas is not—and cannot be—anti-Semitic in the way that a similar portrait would be in the work of a twentieth-century writer. The reason is simply that the typical Elizabethan was unlikely to know very many Jews: the Jews had been expelled from England as long before as 1290, not to be legally readmitted—unless converted to Christianity—until 1656.[13] There were, in fact, a number of Jews, mostly Portuguese and nominally converts, who played a fairly prominent role in

[10] See Leon Kellner, "Die Quelle von Marlowe's 'Jew of Malta,'" *Englische Studien*, X (1887), 80–111; Ethel Seaton, "Fresh Sources for Marlowe," *RES*, V (1929), 385–401; and C. F. Tucker Brooke, "The Prototype of Marlowe's Jew of Malta," *TLS*, June 8, 1922, p. 380.

[11] See A. M. Clark, "*The Jew of Malta*," *Thomas Heywood* (Oxford, 1931), pp. 287–294.

[12] John Bakeless, *The Tragicall History of Christopher Marlowe* (Cambridge, Mass., 1942), 1, 38–41; 334–347.

[13] H. P. Stokes, *A Short History of the Jews in England* (London, 1921), p. 55.

commercial affairs.[14] Londoners, certainly, would have had some knowledge of these people, but that there was any considerable amount of real anti-Jewish feeling is improbable. Indeed, in R. W.'s *The Three Ladies of London*, a play published in 1584, there is an extremely favorable portrayal of a Jew. The Jews were blamed for the Crucifixion, and by a long mediaeval tradition were associated with the Devil and the comic Vice character on the stage, but the prevailing attitude toward them was probably one of fascination and wonder. As J. L. Cardozo puts it, "The favourite foreign country [Italy] was also the most important abode of Jews in the 16th century. The bloody-minded, crafty, extortionate Jew was therefore among the few exotic devices available to produce the foreign atmosphere" in the drama.[15] Charles Knight is close to the truth when he observes in discussing Marlowe's Barabas and Shakespeare's Shylock, "In countries where Jews have abounded and been objects of popular odium, the dramatists who have pandered to prejudice, have uniformly made their Jews mean and ludicrous as well as hateful. Now you may hate Barnabas [*sic*] and Shylock, but you cannot despise them."[16] Perhaps an analogy might be made with the figure of the Indian in Western movies and television plays. Most Americans who watch these productions are not "Indian-haters"; nevertheless, the stereotype—hateful, cruel, inhuman—has been, at least until very recent years, almost universal.

The Machiavelli who introduces *The Jew of Malta* and whose theories Barabas supposedly puts into practice is another such stereotype. Although Niccolò Machiavelli's most influential work, *The Prince*, was not published in English until 1640, translations circulated in manuscript during the later sixteenth century; even earlier, his name had begun to become synonymous with the sort of figure depicted in Marlowe's prologue: an excessively pragmatic, underhanded, treacherous, atheistic, covetous, self-centered, machinating, inhuman monster, such a caricature as is delineated in one of the important sixteenth-century attacks on Machiavelli, Innocent Gentillet's *Discours, sur les moyens de bien gouuerner et maintenir en bonne paix vn royaume ou autre principauté....Contre Nicolas Machiauel Florentin.*

[14] Lucien Wolf, "Jews in Elizabethan England," *Transactions of the Jewish Historical Society of England*, XI (1924–1927), 1–91.

[15] *The Contemporary Jew in the Elizabethan Drama* (Amsterdam, 1925), p. 53.

[16] Charles Knight, ed., *London* (London, 1851), VI, 42.

...[Geneva] 1576. This distortion—vestiges of which linger even today in the popular mind—contributes, like the Maltese setting, the Spanish admiral, the Turkish powers, and the Jew-Devil-Vice tradition, to the exotic and villainous atmosphere which pervades the play, heavily colored though it is with low comedy. The expectations of an Elizabethan audience were conditioned by the very presence of these elements for plots and characterizations of the sort that Marlowe provides; the modern reader, who must also attempt to visualize the play as it was performed at the Rose theater, needs to project himself into the Elizabethan mind, insofar as he can, in order to understand and appreciate *The Jew of Malta* properly.

The play so eludes description that readers have never known quite what to do with it. One seventeenth-century bookseller listed it in his catalogue as a history play; another recorded it as a tragedy in 1661, then changed his mind and decided it was a tragicomedy before issuing another booklist ten years later.[17] If a genre must be found, it is best to admit the paradoxical quality of the play by giving it a paradoxical name and calling it a serious farce.[18] It is, moreover, important to insist that the play does *not* break in two: we do not have a serious play for two acts and a farce for three; rather, the serious and comic elements in the play are present together from the beginning of Act I to the end of Act V, admittedly in varying proportions, but still both present, and present throughout. It would be foolish to deny that Barabas has at the beginning of the play a humanity and dignity that he soon loses; in production, however, the impression of humanity and dignity would not dominate so exclusively as it does when the play is read. Although Barabas' physical appearance is not referred to until later (at II.iii.174 Ithamore says to him, "I worship your nose for this," and at III.iii.10 he calls him a "bottle-nos'd knave"), the prominent facial characteristic still regarded as typically Jewish would—enlarged, distorted, and garishly colored—be apparent to an audience from the moment the play began. Quite possibly the actor who played Barabas would have worn a false red wig as well as the false nose, for both props were traditionally associated with the Jew-Devil-Vice figure. As

[17] Boas, p. 299.

[18] Francis Birrell, "The Jews, or Genius at Play," *New Statesman*, XX (November 11, 1922), 175; T. S. Eliot, "Christopher Marlowe," *Selected Essays* (London, 1932), p. 123; and "*The Jew of Malta* Produced," *Blackwood's Magazine*, CCXII (December, 1922), 833–834.

Kirschbaum shows,[19] the character is also required to have a beard, presumably red and presumably of comic shape and proportions. The opening soliloquy, impressive though its rhetoric is, would leave a decidedly ambivalent first impression if the actor reciting the lines were pawing through his hoard in exaggerated fashion—as I am sure he was meant to do. This comic side of the character is balanced from the beginning, however, first in the ominous prologue delivered by Machiavelli, second in Barabas' very name, taken from the evil criminal in the Gospels who was released to the Jews in preference to Christ, and third by his "humanness," especially in the earlier part of the play.

Reference has already been made to Barabas' association with the Vice tradition of earlier drama; Bernard Spivack's description makes the relationship clear: "The Vice is at once the allegorical aggressor, the homiletic preacher, and the humorist of the moralities—and of plays which, except for his part in them, belong to the later convention of the literal drama."[20] When, however, Spivack later contends that Barabas splits completely into two halves, "a character," "a man," and "a moral figure" in Act I and part of Act II, converted to the Vice by "a change in theatrical method"[21] for the rest of the play, he does less than justice to the skill of Marlowe's dramaturgy, even though it is true that in the later part of the play Barabas loses "emotional caliber, [which is] replaced by a menial alacrity in word and action that is altogether comic. He is too busy with too many murderous contrivances to be distracted by an adequate sense of provocation for any of them."[22] It is perhaps more useful to recall that Barabas stands alone in the role of comic villain for the opening part of the action but that he is joined, in one way or another, by Ithamore, by the two Friars, and by Bellamira and Pilia-Borza—until Barabas has succeeded in killing them all off. Naturally the texture of the play is somewhat different, then, in Acts III and IV.

But only *somewhat* different, for Marlowe brings a basic unity to the play by a variety of other means. On the level of mere plot, the multiplicity of events—despite a few obvious loose ends here and there, such as the confusion over the events antecedent to the duel

[19] Leo Kirschbaum, ed., *The Plays of Christopher Marlowe* (Cleveland, 1962), p. 139.
[20] *Shakespeare and the Allegory of Evil* (New York, 1958), p. 135.
[21] *Ibid.*, p. 348.
[22] *Ibid.*, p. 370.

between Lodowick and Mathias (III.ii) and Bellamira's reference to the siege (III.i.1)—is marvelously well integrated. The first scene prepares us for the introduction of Martin del Bosco and the political plot (ll. 94–96) and initiates the theme of the tribute money due the Turks. I.ii states clearly what was suggested in I.i: Barabas has made careful provision for the contingency that has befallen him. The conversion of his house to a nunnery provides a momentary setback, but his fertile mind soon hits on the scheme of using Abigail as an agent of recovery. The true nature of the Friars is hinted at by their exchange at ll.322–323, and the rivalry between Lodowick and Mathias is prepared for. Out of this skillful exposition in the first act everything else emerges: Barabas' recouping his fortune, Malta's decision to defy the Turks under del Bosco's leadership, the purchase of Ithamore, and the series of revenge plots undertaken by Barabas. His determination to get even with Ferneze accounts for the first of these, the death of Lodowick (and, incidentally, Mathias), and each of the later ones emerges inevitably as part of a campaign to protect himself from disaster: hence the poisoning of Abigail (and, incidentally, the other nuns); the murder of the two Friars, who make the mistake of attempting to capitalize on what they have learned from Abigail; the necessary removal of Ithamore (and, not so incidentally, Bellamira and Pilia-Borza); the alliance with the Turks; and the counterplot with Ferneze where Barabas is finally beaten at his own game. Only the Ithamore-Bellamira-Pilia-Borza episodes are introduced relatively late; even they are got under way at the earliest possible moment, the scene immediately following Barabas' purchase of Ithamore. To trace adequately the careful and complex relationships of these several plots requires nothing short of a full-scale plot summary too long to be attempted here.

Just as important as this skillful structure are the thematic concerns that give a unity to the play. We are a long way from having a world where an avaricious Jew lives; we have instead an avaricious world: when Ferneze (disingenuously) asks of Callapine, "What wind drives you thus into Malta road?" Callapine's reply is not for this play a mere hyperbole: "The wind that bloweth all the world besides:/ Desire of gold" (III.v.3–4). The Turks, the Jews, the Maltese, the Friars, Ithamore, Bellamira, Pilia-Borza—of all the major characters in the play, only Abigail is exempt from materialistic motives. Of the lesser characters, only Mathias and his mother are exceptions; even Lodowick employs the labored diamond metaphor in his conversations with Barabas about Abigail (see especially II.iii.49–69, 293).

In a similar way, the methods of underhanded double-dealing employed by Barabas are also used by characters on all of the various levels of action. The theme is once again introduced through Barabas, but in so subtle a way as to go unnoticed unless one pays close attention. When we first meet him, Barabas is portrayed as almost a type of the commercial magnate, in touch constantly with an operation that moves on a vast scale. Thus in his opening soliloquy and his conversations with the two merchants we see first the skillful businessman, second the miser who is concerned about the quality as well as the quantity of the wealth he amasses (see especially ll.7–37). A further insight into his true character comes in his comparative reflections on Christians:

> Who hateth me but for my happiness?
> Or who is honor'd now but for his wealth?
> Rather had I, a Jew, be hated thus,
> Than pitied in a Christian poverty;
> For I can see no fruits in all their faith,
> But malice, falsehood, and excessive pride,
> Which methinks fits not their profession.
> Happily some hapless man hath conscience,
> And for his conscience lives in beggary.
> They say we are a scatter'd nation:
> I cannot tell, but we have scambled up
> More wealth by far than those that brag of faith.
>
> (I.i.110–121)

Thus before receiving the specific motivation of revenge against Ferneze or anyone else, Barabas is revealed to us as one who despises Christianity—when conscientiously practiced because it brings beggary; when, as it usually is, hypocritically practiced because it is so hypocritical. But Barabas' own hypocrisy and egocentric malice appear immediately in his conversation with the three Jews who come to him for his advice. The aside is a device employed to pyrotechnic effect by Marlowe in this play: Barabas, especially, uses it to reveal his true feelings to the audience, as he does in the first aside in the play (I.i.150–151): "Nay, let 'em combat, conquer, and kill all,/ So they spare me, my daughter, and my wealth." Having made his friends easier in their minds about the visit of the Turks, Barabas begins to plan for the protection of his own interests, revealing as he does so the extent of his self-centeredness and the hypocrisy which he himself is perfectly willing to practice in order to remain secure:

> Howe'er the world go, I'll make sure for one,
> And seek in time to intercept the worst,
> Warily guarding that which I ha' got.
> *Ego mihimet sum semper proximus.*
> Why, let 'em enter, let 'em take the town.
> (I.i.184–188)

We see, then, that Barabas' scorn and hate are directed not only toward the Christians but toward his three fellow Jews, whose interests Barabas has not the slightest intention of protecting. Only his daughter Abigail does he hold exempt from enmity, and she, as the play soon demonstrates, is only an apparent exception: so long as she is as usable and profitable as a bag of portagues, Barabas has the same affection for her that he has for his wealth. Both are pieces of negotiable property. When, however, she takes it upon herself to act as a person in her own right, Barabas' love for her is revealed for what it really is: "For she that varies from me in belief/ Gives great presumption that she loves me not" (III.iv.10–11).

Barabas' unscrupulousness in personal and commercial relations, like all his other characteristics, is particularly noticeable, of course, because he so dominates the play.[23] In his dealings with the lovers, with the Friars, with Ithamore, with the Turks, with Ferneze, with Bellamira and Pilia-Borza, even with Abigail, Barabas is governed by politic considerations. But the focusing of interest on Barabas must not be allowed to obscure the fact that almost everyone else in the play operates on much the same basis: the Turks have intentionally allowed the tribute to pile up in arrears; Ferneze perpetrates the perfectly fraudulent tax arrangement on the three Jews and, even more unfairly, on Barabas; the Maltese decide to defy the Turks but make no pretense of returning the Jews' money to them; del Bosco is at least partially motivated by his wish to sell slaves; one Friar attempts to outdo the other in cleverness as well as in greed; Bellamira and Pilia-Borza play Ithamore for the fool; Ferneze

---

[23] See Harry Levin, *The Overreacher: A Study of Christopher Marlowe* (Cambridge, Mass., 1952), p. 186, where a table credits Barabas with 49 per cent of the lines in the play, the highest percentage of all Marlowe's titular heroes and far above the norm for contemporary plays.

arranges the grand climax, deceiving the Turks and Barabas together. Except for Ithamore—and Marlowe must surely have been smiling to himself—the Turks show up much better, on the whole, than either the Jews or the Christians. But all (save, once again, the much-tried Abigail and a few of the minor characters) operate in terms of *policy*, in its pejorative Elizabethan sense: "In reference to conduct or action generally: Prudent, expedient, or advantageous procedure; prudent or politic course of action; also, as a quality of the agent: sagacity, shrewdness, artfulness; in bad sense, cunning, craftiness, dissimulation" (*OED policy*, I.4.a.). Just as the world of *The Jew of Malta* is a world of avariciousness, so too it is a world of cunning, craftiness, dissimulation—in short, of policy.[24]

To complicate the texture of motives and plots still further, Marlowe employs the device—though it is more than just a device—that was to become the great motif of later Elizabethan and Jacobean tragedy: revenge. We have already seen how Barabas' multiple murders arise out of his need to prevent the discovery of the first two, motivated by revenge. Revenge, moreover, complicates his motives with regard to the Friars and Ithamore; or at least he hauls it in as an excuse. Only in the last scene does he confessedly abandon revenge, having fallen completely in love with policy and the delights that it can bring simply for their own sake:

> Why, is not this
> A kingly kind of trade, to purchase towns
> By treachery, and sell 'em by deceit?
> Now tell me, worldlings, underneath the sun,
> If greater falsehood ever has been done?
> (V.v.46–50)

Earlier in the final act he has at least temporarily forgotten revenge in his obsession with policy and the profit it can bring: "Thus, loving neither, will I live with both,/ Making a profit of my policy" (V.ii. 111–112). But in almost all his operations, revenge lurks as at least an undercurrent of motive. So too, of course, Ferneze and Katherine seek revenge for the deaths of their sons, who had been seeking revenge on each other; Friar Jacomo thinks he is revenging himself on Friar Barnardine; Ithamore justifies his blackmail in part as a means of revenge for Barabas' mistreatment of him; and Ferneze, in the grand

[24] The word *policy* appears thirteen times in the play; see Howard S. Babb, "*Policy* in Marlowe's *The Jew of Malta*," ELH, XXIV (1957), 85–94.

climax of policy, achieves final revenge both on Barabas and on Calymath.

In effect, the play is concerned largely with persons motivated by the basest causes and acting on the basest principles: this world is full of hypocrisy, expedience, greed, and vengeance. As Abigail remarks, "there is no love on earth,/ Pity in Jews, nor piety in Turks" (III.iii.47–48). And yet we must return to the curious ambivalence: *The Jew of Malta* is certainly not a tragedy except insofar as a great many people die in it. It does show a world of evil values and culpable behavior, values and behavior which we are not asked to applaud, though whose power we must perforce respect; but throughout, the rhetoric, the costume and makeup, such conventions as the aside, the comedy of the obscene, the ludicrous, and the merely exaggerated—all combine to make us laugh. Howard S. Babb has put the matter astutely in observing, "The main themes gain in body by being dramatized farcically as well as seriously" and, again, "We are asked to respond seriously to caricature."[25]

This same ambivalence appears, finally, in the styles of the play, infinitely various, but each of indisputable brilliance. As in most Elizabethan verse plays, the norm is a fluid, flexible, workmanlike blank verse that almost any of the Elizabethan dramatists could have written (surely they lisped in numbers). It is remarkably more fluid and flexible than the "mighty line" so often regarded as the epitome of Marlowe's achievement: variation in the placement of the caesura and a relatively frequent use of enjambement give the verse a quality quite unlike that of *Tamburlaine*. The striking passages, those that might be culled out for a collection of anthology pieces, show an even greater brilliance. There are first of all the passages of Marlovian rhetoric, where sounds are piled on sounds, images on images, and rising rhythms on rising rhythms, all combining to produce the effects that only Marlowe is capable of:

> Give me the merchants of the Indian mines,
> That trade in metal of the purest mold;
> The wealthy Moor, that in the eastern rocks
> Without control can pick his riches up,
> And in his house heap pearl like pebble-stones,
> Receive them free, and sell them by the weight,
> Bags of fiery opals, sapphires, amethysts,

25 Pp. 90, 92.

Jacinths, hard topaz, grass-green emeralds,
Beauteous rubies, sparkling diamonds,
And seld-seen costly stones of so great price
As one of them, indifferently rated,
And of a carat of this quantity,
May serve in peril of calamity
To ransom great kings from captivity.

(I.i.19–32)

Such passages, usually appearing in long soliloquies, are counter-pointed by the extremely rapid movement of dialogue that the play incorporates so much of, sometimes (as in I.ii.) with stichomythic effect, sometimes as a rapid-fire comic exchange that both reproduces and parodies the rhythms of everyday speech:[26]

FRIAR BARNARDINE.
　Thy daughter—
FRIAR JACOMO.
　Ay, thy daughter—
BARABAS.
　O, speak not of her; then I die with grief.
FRIAR BARNARDINE.
　Remember that—
FRIAR JACOMO.
　Ay, remember that—
BARABAS.
　I must needs say that I have been a great usurer.
FRIAR BARNARDINE.
　Thou hast committed—
BARABAS.
　Fornication? but that was in another country: and besides,
　the wench is dead.　　　　　　　　　　　　　(IV.i.33–41)

Finally, there are passages of prose as adroit in their manipulation of colloquial inflection as anything that had yet been written in English:

I never knew a man take his death so patiently as this friar.
He was ready to leap off ere the halter was about his neck;
and when the hangman had put on his hempen tippet, he

---

[26] Levin records (p. 187) that the average length of speeches in *The Jew* is only 2.8 lines, whereas *Tamburlaine I* averages 5.9, *Tamburlaine II* 6.3, and even *Doctor Faustus* (1616) 3.6.

made such haste to his prayers as if he had had another
cure to serve. Well, go whither he will, I'll be none of his
followers in haste.   (IV.ii.21–26)

This richness of language in passages skillfully alternated combines
with the richness of episode and of theme to produce a total effect
that is nothing short of dazzling. The play begins slowly, with the
long and dignified set speeches of Barabas in Act I, scene i, moves
more and more rapidly through the ever-increasing tangles of plot
and language in Acts II, III, and IV, and culminates in the intentionally (I would argue) crowded series of climaxes in Act V, where
tables turn so rapidly that the sequence of events is hard to follow.
It might even be argued that this brilliantly theatrical and enter-
taining design is Marlowe's greatest achievement in the play, but
then one remembers that there is also that horrid world of falsity in
political, religious, and personal affairs that is perhaps not so
grotesquely a distortion of reality as, for the sake of humanity, one
might wish.

RICHARD W. VAN FOSSEN

Cornell College

A Note on the Text

The title page of the 1633 quarto of *The Jew of Malta* (*STC* 17412), the only early edition of the play, may be transcribed as follows:

> *The Famous*/ TRAGEDY/ OF/ THE RICH IEVV/ OF *MALTA*./ AS IT WAS PLAYD/ BEFORE THE King AND/ Qveene, IN HIS MAJESTIES/ Theatre at *White-Hall*, by her Majesties/ Servants at the *Cock-pit*./ [rule]/ *Written by* Christopher Marlo./ [rule]/ [ornament]/ *LONDON*;/ Printed by *I. B.* for *Nicholas Vavasour*, and are to be sold/ at his Shop in the Inner-Temple, neere the/ Church. 1633.

I have collated seven copies of this quarto, the three Folger copies and the Newberry (*imp.*) copy in the original, the Harvard, Huntington, and Library of Congress copies in Xerox prints. At least twenty-five other copies have survived. Two press correction variants occur in these seven copies, one each on the inner forme of sheet A and the outer forme of sheet H; the two corrections are recorded at the appropriate points in the textual notes.

The text, printed in the shop of John Beale (I. B.), presents a number of peculiarities, but not enough to solve the problem of revision conclusively.[1] In general, 1633 is a rather ordinary dramatic quarto of the period, somewhat carelessly printed, but with a text that presents few cruces.[2] The quarto occupies thirty-eight leaves, unnumbered: A-I4, K2; A1 (blank) is missing in all three Folger copies, but Greg records one copy in which it has been preserved.[3] The title appears on A2, the verso of which is blank, preliminary matter occupies A3–A4v, and the text of the play, beginning with the

[1] I am deeply indebted to Mr. Robert Welsh of Duke University for discussing with me his investigation of the text of *The Jew of Malta*, but his conclusions do not always agree with mine. See his Duke University doctoral dissertation (Durham, N.C., 1963).

[2] See J. C. Maxwell, "How Bad Is the Text of 'The Jew of Malta'?" *MLR*, XLVIII (1953), 435–438.

[3] W. W. Greg, *A Bibliography of the English Printed Drama to the Restoration* (London, 1939–1959), II, 625 (item 475).

Machiavelli prologue, starts on B. One skeleton is used for sheets B and C, two for the rest of the book, alternating in a regular pattern, the whole set by one compositor. Robert Welsh has collected evidence of broken types to suggest that the quarto was set by formes, the inner first.

One peculiarity that may be noticed from the transcription of the title page is the occurrence of internal *v* thirty times where most early seventeenth-century texts employ *u*. I have examined six other dramatic quartos printed in Beale's shop during the period 1632–1634 and find this anomaly common to all, usually with greater frequency than in *The Jew of Malta*.[4] An analogous form, initial *u*, appears six times in *The Jew*.

A few spelling peculiarities present difficulties. *The Jew* frequently uses *'em* (twice *'vm*) for *them*, *ha* for *have*, and *wud* for *would*; these forms are almost nonexistent in Marlowe's other plays, but the contractions, at least, are of a nature that implies authorial or scribal rather than printing house origin; the evidence of the other Beale quartos, moreover, suggests that the compositors were following copy. We are forced to conclude from this particular evidence, then, either that the manuscript from which the quarto was printed was revised or corrected by someone other than Marlowe or that Marlowe changed his spelling of these words for this one play. This latter alternative, in view of the colloquial quality of *The Jew of Malta*, quite unlike most of Marlowe's other work, is not so improbable as it might appear at first. A few spellings characteristic of Heywood appear: *oa* for *o* (*choake* and others), *dg* for *g* (*sindg'd*), and *bloud* for *blood*. They are, however, very few, almost all of them appear, curiously enough, in the parts of the play unanimously attributed to Marlowe, and the *oa*, at least, can be found in most of the other Beale quartos. One possible conclusion, though extremely doubtful, might be that Heywood made a transcription of Marlowe's manuscript. Nevertheless, this relatively infrequent appearance of Heywood spellings, when taken together with Fräulein Thimme's study of meter, diction, and syntax (uniform throughout the play), Bennett's conclusions about vocabulary (Marlovian, not Heywoodian), and

4 Shakerley Marmion, *Holland's Leaguer*, 1632; Philip Massinger, *The Maid of Honor*, 1632; Thomas Goffe, *The Tragedy of Orestes*, 1633; John Ford, *The Broken Heart*, 1633; John Ford, *Love's Sacrifice*, 1633; Samuel Rowley? *The Noble Soldier*, 1634.

Taylor's analysis of Marlowe's predilection for the word *now* (sixty-seven times in *The Jew of Malta*, often in the "suspect" scenes), makes it seem extremely unlikely that Heywood or anyone else revised the play to any great extent.[5]

Whoever wrote or transcribed the manuscript that served as copy for the quarto, inconsistencies in speech-tags suggest authorial rather than theatrical origin. In I.i the speech-tag for Barabas is uniformly *Iew.*, those for the other three Jews simply *1.*, *2.*, and *3.* (*1 Iew.* and *2 Iew.* in I.ii); elsewhere, *Bar.* is the usual prefix for Barabas. The tag for the first merchant (I.i) is *Merch.*, that for the second merchant usually *2. Merch.*, once simply *Merch.* Friars Jacomo and Barnardine are *1 Fry.* and *2 Fry.* throughout, save in IV.i, where we have *Iocoma* in a stage direction and *Ioco.* in speech-tags. In II.iii the speeches of the unnamed slave are given to Ithamore. There are several generic attributions: Bellamira appears throughout as *Curtezane* and *Curt.*, Ferneze as *Gouernor* and *Gouer.* or *Gov.*, Katherine as *Mater*, and Callapine as *1 Bass.* In I.ii, the officer who reads the document is identified in the speech-tags as *Reader* and *Read.* In the same scene, the first three speeches of the Abbess are assigned to *1 Nun.*, *Nun.*, and *Abb.* One inconsistency of special interest is the variation in the title of Calymath's lieutenants: in I.ii, they are Bassoes (also the spelling in *Tamburlaine* I and II) in the text and stage directions; in the later part of the play they are called Bashawes, the more usual Elizabethan form. This particular peculiarity might well be used to support the view that someone other than Marlowe reworked the last part of the play. Similarly, the confusion arising from the plural governors of Malta in I.ii and the singular that prevails elsewhere might be interpreted as suggesting revision.

[5] Margarete Thimme, *Marlowe's "Jew of Malta": Stil- und Echtheitsfragen* (Halle, 1921); H. S. Bennett, ed., *The Jew of Malta and The Massacre at Paris* (London, 1931), pp. 8–9; George Coffin Taylor, "Marlowe's Now," *Elizabethan Studies and Other Essays in Honor of George F. Reynolds* (Boulder, 1945), pp. 93–100.

List of Editions

LIST OF EDITIONS

Griffin	B. Griffin, ed., *The Jew of Malta.* Williamstown, 1909.
Thomas	Edward Thomas, ed., *The Plays of Christopher Marlowe.* London, 1909. (Everyman's Library.)
Brooke 1	C. F. T. Brooke, ed., *The Works of Christopher Marlowe.* Oxford, 1910.
Neilson	W. A. Neilson, ed., *The Chief Elizabethan Dramatists.* Boston, 1911.
Phelps	William Lyon Phelps, ed., *Christopher Marlowe.* New York, 1912.
Bennett	H. S. Bennett, ed., *"The Jew of Malta" and "The Massacre at Paris."* London, 1931.
Spencer	Hazelton Spencer, ed., *Elizabethan Plays.* Boston, 1933.
Brooke 2	C. F. T. Brooke and N. B. Paradise, eds., *English Drama, 1580–1642.* Boston, 1933.
Parks	E. W. Parks and R. C. Beatty, eds., *The English Drama: An Anthology, 900–1642.* New York, 1935.
World	*The Plays of Christopher Marlowe.* London, 1939. (World's Classics.)
Ridley	M. R. Ridley, ed., *Plays and Poems of Christopher Marlowe.* London, 1955. (Everyman's Library.)
Kirschbaum	Leo Kirschbaum, ed., *The Plays of Christopher Marlowe.* Cleveland, 1962.
Ribner	Irving Ribner, ed., *The Complete Plays of Christopher Marlowe.* New York, 1963.

THE JEW OF MALTA

The Epistle Dedicatory
to My Worthy Friend, Master Thomas Hammon,
of Gray's Inn, &c.

This play, composed by so worthy an author as Master
Marlowe, and the part of the Jew presented by so unimitable
an actor as Master Alleyn, being in this later age commended
to the stage, as I usher'd it unto the Court, and presented it
to the Cock-pit, with these Prologues and Epilogues here   5
inserted, so now being newly brought to the press, I was
loath it should be published without the ornament of an
Epistle, making choice of you unto whom to devote it, than
whom (of all those gentlemen and acquaintance within
the compass of my long knowledge) there is none more able   10
to tax ignorance or attribute right to merit. Sir, you have
been pleased to grace some of mine own works with your
courteous patronage; I hope this will not be the worse
accepted because commended by me, over whom none can
claim more power or privilege than yourself. I had no   15
better a New Year's gift to present you with; receive it

0.1. The...Dedicatory] *from the*
running-title to A3v Q.

0.2. *Thomas Hammon*] Heywood also dedicated the second part of *The
Fair Maid of the West* (1631) and the first part of *The Iron Age* (1632) to him;
in the former the playwright refers to him as "the true favorer of the muses,
and all good arts."

0.3. *Gray's Inn*] one of the Inns of Court, societies of lawyers and law
schools.

2. *unimitable*] inimitable.

3. *Alleyn*] Edward Alleyn (1566–1626), one of the most famous actors
of the day, especially during his career with the Lord Admiral's company
in the 1590's.

4. *usher'd it unto*] introduced it to.

5. *Cock-pit*] a "private" (indoor) theater in Drury Lane, opened in 1617;
also known as The Phoenix, it was used for theatrical purposes even after
the Restoration.

8. *devote it*] dedicate it formally.

11. *tax*] blame, censure.

11. *right*] just due.

13. *patronage*] favor.

therefore as a continuance of that inviolable obligement by which he rests still engaged who, as he ever hath, shall always remain,

Tuissimus,   20
THO. HEYWOOD

---

20. *Tuissimus*] wholly thine.

The Prologue Spoken at Court

Gracious and great, that we so boldly dare
('Mongst other plays that now in fashion are)
To present this, writ many years agone,
And in that age, thought second unto none,
We humbly crave your pardon; we pursue   5
The story of a rich and famous Jew
Who liv'd in Malta. You shall find him still,
In all his projects, a sound Machevill;
And that's his character. He that hath past
So many censures, is now come at last   10
To have your princely ears. Grace you him; then
You crown the action, and renown the pen.

5. pardon] *Q corr.;* parpon *Q
uncorr.*

---

1. *Gracious and great*] i.e., the king and queen.
5. *pursue*] trace.
8. *sound*] thorough, solid.
10. *censures*] judgments, criticisms.

The Prologue to the Stage, at the Cock-pit

We know not how our play may pass this stage,
Marlowe But by the best of poets in that age
The *Malta Jew* had being, and was made;
Alleyn And he, then by the best of actors play'd.
In *Hero and Leander*, one did gain   5
A lasting memory; in *Tamburlaine*,
This *Jew*, with others many, th' other wan
The attribute of peerless, being a man
Whom we may rank with (doing no one wrong)
Proteus for shapes, and Roscius for a tongue,   10
So could he speak, so vary; nor is 't hate
Perkins To merit in him who doth personate
Our Jew this day, nor is it his ambition
To exceed, or equal, being of condition
More modest; this is all that he intends   15
(And that, too, at the urgence of some friends):
To prove his best, and if none here gainsay it,
The part he hath studied, and intends to play it.

---

4. *best of actors*] see note to Epistle Dedicatory, l.3, above; Alleyn played the title role in *Tamburlaine*, Marlowe's first great success on the stage.

5. *Hero and Leander*] erotic narrative poem, a paraphrase of Musaeus, begun by Marlowe and completed by George Chapman; published 1598.

7. *wan*] won.

10. *Proteus*] in Greek mythology, a minor sea-god with the power to take any shape; hence an appropriate compliment to an actor.

10. *Roscius*] Quintus Roscius Gallus (d. 62 B.C.), most famous of Roman comedians, the type of a perfect actor.

11-12. *hate/ To merit*] i.e., professional jealousy.

12. *him*] Richard Perkins, one of the most famous actors of his day; his career extended (at least) from 1602 to 1637.

14. *condition*] character, temper, cast of mind.

16. *urgence*] pressing solicitation.

17. *prove*] try.

17. *gainsay*] hinder, oppose.

[Dramatis Personae

FERNEZE, *Governor of Malta*
LODOWICK, *his son*
SELIM CALYMATH, *son of the Emperor of Turkey*
MARTIN DEL BOSCO, *Vice-Admiral of Spain*
MATHIAS, *a gentleman*
BARABAS, *the Jew of Malta*
ITHAMORE, *his slave*
CALLAPINE, *bashaw to Calymath*
FRIAR JACOMO
FRIAR BARNARDINE
PILIA-BORZA, *a bully*
TWO MERCHANTS
THREE JEWS
KNIGHTS OF MALTA, BASHAWS, OFFICERS, FRIARS, SLAVES,
    GUARD, MESSENGER, ATTENDANTS, CARPENTERS

KATHERINE, *mother to Mathias*
ABIGAIL, *daughter to Barabas*
BELLAMIRA, *a courtesan*
ABBESS
NUN

MACHIAVEL, *speaker of the Prologue*]

The Jew of Malta

[*Prologue*]   [*Enter*] Machiavel.

MACHIAVEL.
   Albeit the world think Machiavel is dead,
   Yet was his soul but flown beyond the Alps,
   And, now the Guise is dead, is come from France,
   To view this land, and frolic with his friends.
   To some, perhaps, my name is odious,   5
   But such as love me, guard me from their tongues,
   And let them know that I am Machiavel,
   And weigh not men, and therefore not men's words.
   Admir'd I am of those that hate me most:
   Though some speak openly against my books,   10
   Yet will they read me, and thereby attain
   To Peter's chair; and when they cast me off,
   Are poison'd by my climbing followers.
   I count religion but a childish toy,
   And hold there is no sin but ignorance.   15
   Birds of the air will tell of murders past;

0.1. Machiavel] *Reed; Macheuil Q;*
so also (with two l's) in ll. 1 and 7.

2.] "i.e. the soul of Machiavelli had suffered metamorphosis into that
of Guise." (Bennett).

3. *Guise*] Henri de Lorraine, 3rd Duke of Guise (1550–1588), Roman
Catholic nobleman and politician, who directed the infamous massacre of
Protestants on St. Bartholomew's Day (August 24) 1572; for the English a
type of the Machiavellian villain-politician.

4. *friends*] i.e., "the English devotees of Machiavellian policy" (Brooke).

6. *guard*] protect.

6. *their tongues*] the tongues of my enemies.

8. *weigh*] esteem, attach importance to.

9. *Admir'd*] wondered at.   9. *of*] by.

12. *Peter's chair*] i.e., the Papacy.

14. *toy*] trifle.

16.] according to Greek legend, the murderers of Ibycus were brought
to justice by means of a flock of cranes.

I am asham'd to hear such fooleries.
Many will talk of title to a crown;
What right had Caesar to the empire?
Might first made kings, and laws were then most sure   20
When, like the Draco's, they were writ in blood.
Hence comes it, that a strong-built citadel
Commands much more than letters can import.
Which maxim had Phalaris observ'd,
H' had never bellowed in a brazen bull   25
Of great ones' envy; o' th' poor, petty wights,
Let me be envied and not pitied!
But whither am I bound? I come not, I,
To read a lecture here in Britain,
But to present the tragedy of a Jew,   30
Who smiles to see how full his bags are cramm'd,
Which money was not got without my means.
I crave but this: grace him as he deserves,
And let him not be entertain'd the worse
Because he favors me.   [*Exit.*]   35

[I.i]

    Enter Barabas *in his countinghouse, with heaps of gold before him.*

BARABAS.

    So that of thus much that return was made:
    And of the third part of the Persian ships,
    There was the venture summ'd and satisfied.

21. Draco's] *Reed; Drancus Q.*   *elsewhere act but not scene divisions are*
I.i. 0.1.] *no scene division in Q;* *indicated.*

---

    21. *Draco*] Athenian legislator, codifier of a proverbially severe legal
code.
    24. *Phalaris*] tyrant (ruler) of Acragas, in Sicily, for whom was made a
brazen bull in which he roasted his enemies; one tradition says that he was
overthrown and killed in his own device.
    26. *wights*] people.   33. *grace*] honor.
    34. *entertain'd*] received (as a guest).
    35. *favors*] (1) sides with (2) resembles.
[I.i]
    0.1. *Barabas*] the name of the prisoner released to the Jews instead of
Jesus; see Matthew 27 : 15–26.
    3. *summ'd*] brought to completion.   3. *satisfied*] fully paid.

As for those Scenites, and the men of Uz,
That bought my Spanish oils, and wines of Greece,   5
Here have I purs'd their paltry silverlings.
Fie! what a trouble 'tis to count this trash.
Well fare the Arabians, who so richly pay
The things they traffic for with wedge of gold,
Whereof a man may easily in a day   10
Tell that which may maintain him all his life.
The needy groom, that never finger'd groat,
Would make a miracle of thus much coin;
But he whose steel-barr'd coffers are cramm'd full,
And all his lifetime hath been tired,   15
Wearing his fingers' ends with telling it,
Would in his age be loath to labor so,
And for a pound to sweat himself to death.
Give me the merchants of the Indian mines,
That trade in metal of the purest mold;   20
The wealthy Moor, that in the eastern rocks
Without control can pick his riches up,
And in his house heap pearl like pebble-stones,
Receive them free, and sell them by the weight,
Bags of fiery opals, sapphires, amethysts,   25
Jacinths, hard topaz, grass-green emeralds,
Beauteous rubies, sparkling diamonds,
And seld-seen costly stones of so great price
As one of them, indifferently rated,
And of a carat of this quantity,   30

---

4. Scenites] *conj. Seaton;* Samintes *Q.*   25. amethysts] *Reed;* Amatists *Q.*
6. silverlings] *conj. Reed;* siluerbings   30. carat] *Robinson;* Carrect *Q.*
Q.

---

4. *Scenites*] poor Arabian nomads (Seaton).
4. *Uz*] country near Palestine, the home of Job; see Job 1:1.
6. *silverlings*] shekels, small coins; see Isaiah 7:23.
7. *trash*] contemptuous term for money in Elizabethan slang.
8. *Well fare the Arabians*] may the Arabians fare well.
9. *traffic*] bargain, deal.
9. *wedge*] ingot.   11. *Tell*] count.
12. *groom*] servant.
12. *groat*] coin worth fourpence.
22. *Without control*] freely.   28. *seld-seen*] seldom seen.
29. *indifferently rated*] impartially valued.

May serve in peril of calamity
To ransom great kings from captivity.
This is the ware wherein consists my wealth:
And thus methinks should men of judgment frame
Their means of traffic from the vulgar trade,   35
And as their wealth increaseth, so enclose
Infinite riches in a little room.
But now how stands the wind?
Into what corner peers my halcyon's bill?
Ha! to the east? yes: see how stands the vanes?   40
East and by south. Why then I hope my ships
I sent for Egypt and the bordering isles
Are gotten up by Nilus' winding banks:
Mine argosy from Alexandria,
Loaden with spice and silks, now under sail,   45
Are smoothly gliding down by Candy shore
To Malta, through our Mediterranean sea.
But who comes here? How now?

Enter a Merchant.

I MERCHANT.

Barabas, thy ships are safe,
Riding in Malta road; and all the merchants   50
With other merchandise are safe arriv'd,
And have sent me to know whether yourself
Will come and custom them.

BARABAS.

The ships are safe, thou say'st, and richly fraught?

---

34. *frame*] construct.
35. *traffic*] commerce.
35. *from*] away from.
39. *halcyon*] the kingfisher; its dead body, hung up by the bill, supposedly
indicated the direction of the wind.
40. *vanes*] weather vanes.
44. *argosy*] largest size of merchant ship.
46. *Candy*] Candia, the Italian name for Crete.
50. *road*] "a sheltered piece of water near the shore where vessels may
lie at anchor in safety" (*OED*).
53. *custom them*] pass them through the customhouse.
54. *fraught*] laden.

1 MERCHANT.

    They are.

BARABAS.   Why then go bid them come ashore,   55
    And bring with them their bills of entry:
    I hope our credit in the customhouse
    Will serve as well as I were present there.
    Go send 'em threescore camels, thirty mules,
    And twenty wagons to bring up the ware.   60
    But art thou master in a ship of mine,
    And is thy credit not enough for that?

1 MERCHANT.

    The very custom barely comes to more
    Than many merchants of the town are worth,
    And therefore far exceeds my credit, sir.   65

BARABAS.

    Go tell 'em the Jew of Malta sent thee, man:
    Tush, who amongst 'em knows not Barabas?

1 MERCHANT.

    I go.

BARABAS.   So then, there's somewhat come. Sirrah,
    Which of my ships art thou master of?

1 MERCHANT.

    Of the *Speranza*, sir.

BARABAS.   And saw'st thou not   70
    Mine argosy at Alexandria?
    Thou couldst not come from Egypt, or by Caire,
    But at the entry there into the sea
    Where Nilus pays his tribute to the main;
    Thou needs must sail by Alexandria.   75

1 MERCHANT.

    I neither saw them, nor inquir'd of them.
    But this we heard some of our seamen say,
    They wonder'd how you durst with so much wealth
    Trust such a crazed vessel, and so far.

---

58. *as I*] as if I.
63. *The very custom barely*] the mere duty.
68. *Sirrah*] "ordinary form of address to inferiors" (Onions).
72. *Caire*] Cairo.   79. *crazed*] damaged.

BARABAS.

    Tush; they are wise! I know her and her strength.   80

    Bye, go, go thou thy ways, discharge thy ship,

    And bid my factor bring his loading in.   [*Exit* 1 Merchant.]

    And yet I wonder at this argosy.

Enter a second Merchant.

2 MERCHANT.

    Thine argosy from Alexandria,

    Know, Barabas, doth ride in Malta road,   85

    Laden with riches, and exceeding store

    Of Persian silks, of gold, and orient pearl.

BARABAS.

    How chance you came not with those other ships

    That sail'd by Egypt?

2 MERCHANT.   Sir, we saw 'em not.

BARABAS.

    Belike they coasted round by Candy shore   90

    About their oils, or other businesses.

    But 'twas ill done of you to come so far

    Without the aid or conduct of their ships.

2 MERCHANT.

    Sir, we were wafted by a Spanish fleet

    That never left us till within a league,   95

    That had the galleys of the Turk in chase.

BARABAS.

    O, they were going up to Sicily. Well, go

    And bid the merchants and my men dispatch

81. Bye] *Reed;* By *Q.*

---

    80. *Tush*] "an exclamation of impatient contempt or disparagement" (*OED*).

    80. *they are wise*] i.e., "a lot they know about it."

    81. *discharge*] unload.

    82. *factor*] mercantile agent.   82. *loading*] bill of lading.

    86. *exceeding*] extremely great.   87. *orient*] precious.

    90. *Belike*] probably.   90. *coasted*] sailed along the coast.

    94. *wafted*] convoyed.   95. *league*] about three miles.

    98. *dispatch*] be quick.

And come ashore, and see the fraught discharg'd.

2 MERCHANT.

I go.   *Exit.* 100

BARABAS.

Thus trolls our fortune in by land and sea,
And thus are we on every side enrich'd:
These are the blessings promis'd to the Jews,
And herein was old Abram's happiness.
What more may heaven do for earthly man   105
Than thus to pour out plenty in their laps,
Ripping the bowels of the earth for them,
Making the sea their servants, and the winds
To drive their substance with successful blasts?
Who hateth me but for my happiness?   110
Or who is honor'd now but for his wealth?
Rather had I, a Jew, be hated thus,
Than pitied in a Christian poverty;
For I can see no fruits in all their faith,
But malice, falsehood, and excessive pride,   115
Which methinks fits not their profession.
Happily some hapless man hath conscience,
And for his conscience lives in beggary.
They say we are a scatter'd nation:
I cannot tell, but we have scambled up   120
More wealth by far than those that brag of faith.
There's Kirriah Jairim, the great Jew of Greece,

101. trolls] *Dyce 2;* trowles *Q.*

---

99. *fraught*] cargo.
101. *trolls*] comes "in abundantly like a flowing stream" (*OED*).
103.] see Genesis 15 : 14.
104. *Abram*] Abraham.   109. *substance*] goods.
109. *successful*] propitious.
114.] compare the words of Christ, Matthew 7 : 20: "Wherefore by their fruits ye shall know them."
116. *their profession*] the faith they profess.
117. *Happily*] perhaps.
117. *hapless*] unlucky.
120. *scambled up*] scrambled together in haphazard fashion.
122. *Kirriah Jairim*] Kiriath Jearim, a border town of Palestine, is mentioned in 1 Chronicles 2 in such a way as to make it sound like a personal name (Koeppel).

Obed in Bairseth, Nones in Portugal,
Myself in Malta, some in Italy,
Many in France, and wealthy every one: 125
Ay, wealthier far than any Christian.
I must confess we come not to be kings;
That's not our fault: alas, our number's few,
And crowns come either by succession
Or urg'd by force; and nothing violent,   130
Oft have I heard tell, can be permanent.
Give us a peaceful rule; make Christians kings,
That thirst so much for principality.
I have no charge, nor many children,
But one sole daughter, whom I hold as dear   135
As Agamemnon did his Iphigen;
And all I have is hers. But who comes here?

Enter three Jews.

1 JEW.
Tush, tell not me 'twas done of policy.
2 JEW.
Come, therefore, let us go to Barabas,
For he can counsel best in these affairs;   140
And here he comes.
BARABAS.   Why, how now, countrymen?
Why flock you thus to me in multitudes?
What accident's betided to the Jews?

---

123. *Obed*] in Old Testament history, father of Jesse; also mentioned in 1 Chronicles 2.

123. *Bairseth*] unidentified.

123. *Nones*] a Portuguese Jewess, Maria Nuñes, impressed Queen Elizabeth, and Dr. Hector Nunez, an important Portuguese Jew, was in London (Bennett).

130. *urg'd by force*] forcibly gained.

133. *principality*] sovereignty.

134. *charge*] burden of responsibility.

136. *Agamemnon . . . Iphigen*] the Greek leader Agamemnon, on his way to the Trojan war, offended Artemis and, in order to appease her, had to sacrifice his daughter Iphigenia; he did so.

138. *policy*] a key word in the play; here, "statecraft," "prudence in the management of affairs" (Onions); often, "deceitful underhand method of procedure" (Bennett).

1 JEW.

　　A fleet of warlike galleys, Barabas,
　　Are come from Turkey, and lie in our road;   145
　　And they this day sit in the council-house
　　To entertain them and their embassy.

BARABAS.

　　Why, let 'em come, so they come not to war;
　　Or let 'em war, so we be conquerors.
　　(aside) Nay, let 'em combat, conquer, and kill all,   150
　　So they spare me, my daughter, and my wealth.

1 JEW.

　　Were it for confirmation of a league,
　　They would not come in warlike manner thus.

2 JEW.

　　I fear their coming will afflict us all.

BARABAS.

　　Fond men, what dream you of their multitudes?   155
　　What need they treat of peace that are in league?
　　The Turks and those of Malta are in league.
　　Tut, tut; there is some other matter in 't.

1 JEW.

　　Why, Barabas, they come for peace or war.

BARABAS.

　　Happily for neither, but to pass along   160
　　Towards Venice by the Adriatic sea,
　　With whom they have attempted many times,
　　But never could effect their stratagem.

3 JEW.

　　And very wisely said; it may be so.

2 JEW.

　　But there's a meeting in the senate-house,   165
　　And all the Jews in Malta must be there.

BARABAS.

　　Hum; all the Jews in Malta must be there?
　　Ay, like enough; why then let every man

167. Hum] *Reed;* Vmh Q.

147. *embassy*] message committed to an ambassador.
155. *Fond*] foolish.　　160. *Happily*] perhaps.
162. *With*] against.　　162. *attempted*] made attacks.

Provide him, and be there for fashion sake.
If anything shall there concern our state,   170
Assure yourselves I'll look unto—(*aside*) myself.

1 JEW.
    I know you will; well, brethren, let us go.
2 JEW.
    Let's take our leaves; farewell, good Barabas.
BARABAS.
    Do so; farewell, Zaareth, farewell, Temainte.   [*Exeunt* Jews.]
    And, Barabas, now search this secret out.   175
    Summon thy senses, call thy wits together:
    These silly men mistake the matter clean.
    Long to the Turk did Malta contribute,
    Which tribute—all in policy, I fear—
    The Turks have let increase to such a sum   180
    As all the wealth of Malta cannot pay;
    And now by that advantage thinks, belike,
    To seize upon the town. Ay, that he seeks.
    Howe'er the world go, I'll make sure for one,
    And seek in time to intercept the worst,   185
    Warily guarding that which I ha' got.
    Ego mihimet sum semper proximus.
    Why, let 'em enter, let 'em take the town.   [*Exit.*]

[I.ii]
Enter [Ferneze,] *Governors of Malta* (Knights) [*, and* Officers,] *met by*
[Callapine *and other*] *Bashaws of the Turk* [*and*] Calymath.

FERNEZE.
    Now, bashaws, what demand you at our hands?

---

187. *proximus*] *Reed; proximas Q.*

---

    169. *Provide him*] make himself ready.
    169. *for fashion sake*] "as a formality" (Bennett).   170. *state*] welfare.
    174. *Zaareth*] the name of a Persian lady at a Persian court (Hurwitz).
    174. *Temainte*] Eliphaz, one of Job's friends, was a member of the Temanite tribe.
    177. *silly*] stupid.   177. *clean*] completely.   185. *intercept*] prevent.
    187.] misquoted from Terence's *Andria*, IV.i.12: *proximus sum egomet mihi*—"no man is nearer friend to myself than I am" (Cooper).
[I.ii]
    0.1. *Governors of Malta (Knights)*] in this scene Marlowe seems to assume plural governors of Malta; the parenthesis does not appear in the quarto.
    0.2. *Bashaws*] pashas; military title for high Turkish officials.

-17-

CALLAPINE.

    Know, Knights of Malta, that we came from Rhodes,
    From Cyprus, Candy, and those other isles
    That lie betwixt the Mediterranean seas.

FERNEZE.

    What's Cyprus, Candy, and those other isles   5
    To us, or Malta? What at our hands demand ye?

CALYMATH.

    The ten years' tribute that remains unpaid.

FERNEZE.

    Alas, my lord, the sum is overgreat;
    I hope your Highness will consider us.

CALYMATH.

    I wish, grave governors, 'twere in my power   10
    To favor you, but 'tis my father's cause,
    Wherein I may not, nay, I dare not dally.

FERNEZE.

    Then give us leave, great Selim Calymath.

CALYMATH [to the bashaws].

    Stand all aside, and let the knights determine—
    And send to keep our galleys under sail,   15
    For happily we shall not tarry here.
    [to the Maltese] Now, governors, how are you resolv'd?

FERNEZE.

    Thus: since your hard conditions are such
    That you will needs have ten years' tribute past,
    We may have time to make collection   20
    Amongst the inhabitants of Malta for 't.

CALLAPINE.

    That's more than is in our commission.

CALYMATH.

    What, Callapine, a little courtesy!
    Let's know their time. Perhaps it is not long;
    And 'tis more kingly to obtain by peace   25

---

    2. *Knights of Malta*] Knights of St. John of Jerusalem, whose head-
quarters were on Malta.
    10. *grave*] honored; "an epithet of respectful address" (*OED*).
    13. *give us leave*] permit us (to confer apart).
    15. *send*] send word.   19. *needs*] of necessity.

Than to enforce conditions by constraint.
What respite ask you, governors?

FERNEZE.   But a month.

CALYMATH.

We grant a month, but see you keep your promise.
Now launch our galleys back again to sea,
Where we'll attend the respite you have ta'en,   30
And for the money send our messenger.
Farewell, great governors, and brave Knights of Malta.

                    Exeunt [Calymath, Callapine, *and Bashaws*].

FERNEZE.

And all good fortune wait on Calymath.
Go, one, and call those Jews of Malta hither:
Were they not summon'd to appear today?   35

I OFFICER.

They were, my lord, and here they come.

                    Enter Barabas *and three* Jews.

I KNIGHT.

Have you determin'd what to say to them?

FERNEZE.

Yes, give me leave; and, Hebrews, now come near.
From the Emperor of Turkey is arriv'd
Great Selim Calymath, his Highness' son,   40
To levy of us ten years' tribute past;
Now then, here know that it concerneth us—

BARABAS.

Then, good my lord, to keep your quiet still,
Your lordship shall do well to let them have it.

FERNEZE.

Soft, Barabas, there's more 'longs to 't than so.   45
To what this ten years' tribute will amount,
That we have cast, but cannot compass it
By reason of the wars, that robb'd our store;
And therefore are we to request your aid.

BARABAS.

Alas, my lord, we are no soldiers: 50

---

27. *respite*] delay.   30. *attend*] wait for.   33. *wait on*] attend.
43. *quiet*] "peaceful condition of affairs" (*OED*).
45. *'longs*] belongs.   47. *cast*] calculated.   47. *compass*] attain.

And what's our aid against so great a prince?

1 KNIGHT.

Tut, Jew, we know thou art no soldier;
Thou art a merchant, and a moneyed man,
And 'tis thy money, Barabas, we seek.

BARABAS.

How, my lord, my money?

FERNEZE.   Thine and the rest;   55
For, to be short, amongst you 't must be had.

1 JEW.

Alas, my lord, the most of us are poor.

FERNEZE.

Then let the rich increase your portions.

BARABAS.

Are strangers with your tribute to be tax'd?

2 KNIGHT.

Have strangers leave with us to get their wealth?   60
Then let them with us contribute.

BARABAS.

How, equally?

FERNEZE.   No, Jew, like infidels.
For through our sufferance of your hateful lives,
Who stand accursed in the sight of heaven,
These taxes and afflictions are befall'n,   65
And therefore thus we are determined:
Read there the articles of our decrees.

1 OFFICER [*reading*].

First, the tribute money of the Turks shall all be levied
amongst the Jews, and each of them to pay one half of his
estate.   70

BARABAS.

How, half his estate? I hope you mean not mine!

FERNEZE.

Read on.

1 OFFICER [*reading*].

Secondly, he that denies to pay, shall straight become a
Christian.

---

59. *strangers*] foreigners.
73. *denies*] refuses.   73. *straight*] immediately.

BARABAS.

How! a Christian! Hum, what's here to do?   75

1 OFFICER [*reading*].

Lastly, he that denies this, shall absolutely lose all he has.

ALL 3 JEWS.

O, my lord, we will give half.

BARABAS.

O, earth-mettl'd villains, and no Hebrews born!
And will you basely thus submit yourselves
To leave your goods to their arbitrament?   80

FERNEZE.

Why, Barabas, wilt thou be christen'd?

BARABAS.

No, governor, I will be no convertite.

FERNEZE.

Then pay thy half.

BARABAS.

Why, know you what you did by this device?
Half of my substance is a city's wealth.   85
Governor, it was not got so easily;
Nor will I part so slightly therewithal.

FERNEZE.

Sir, half is the penalty of our decree;
Either pay that, or we will seize on all.

[*Exeunt* Officers, *on a sign from* Ferneze.]

BARABAS.

Corpo di Dio! stay: you shall have half;   90
Let me be us'd but as my brethren are.

FERNEZE.

No, Jew, thou hast denied the articles,
And now it cannot be recall'd.

90. *Dio*] *Collier; deo Q.*

---

75. *How!*] what!
78. *earth-mettl'd*] "ignominious, endued with earthly mettle or spirit"
(Bennett).
80. *arbitrament*] absolute control.   82. *convertite*] convert.
84. *device*] trick.   85. *substance*] possessions, wealth.
87. *slightly*] easily.
88. *penalty*] fine.
90. *Corpo di Dio*] body of God.

BARABAS.

    Will you then steal my goods?

    Is theft the ground of your religion?   95

FERNEZE.

    No, Jew, we take particularly thine

    To save the ruin of a multitude:

    And better one want for a common good,

    Than many perish for a private man.

    Yet, Barabas, we will not banish thee,   100

    But here in Malta, where thou gott'st thy wealth,

    Live still; and, if thou canst, get more.

BARABAS.

    Christians—what, or how can I multiply?

    Of naught is nothing made.

1 KNIGHT.

    From naught at first thou cam'st to little wealth,   105

    From little unto more, from more to most:

    If your first curse fall heavy on thy head,

    And make thee poor and scorn'd of all the world,

    'Tis not our fault, but thy inherent sin.

BARABAS.

    What? bring you scripture to confirm your wrongs?   110

    Preach me not out of my possessions.

    Some Jews are wicked, as all Christians are:

    But say the tribe that I descended of

    Were all in general cast away for sin,

    Shall I be tried by their transgression?   115

    The man that dealeth righteously shall live:

    And which of you can charge me otherwise?

FERNEZE.

    Out, wretched Barabas!

    Sham'st thou not thus to justify thyself

---

95. *ground*] fundamental principle, basis.

96. *particularly*] individually.   97. *save*] avoid.

98. *want*] lack.   98–99.] see John 11 : 50.

99. *private*] individual.   103. *multiply*] increase in wealth.

107.] see Matthew 27 : 25.

114. *in general*] collectively, without exception.

114. *cast away*] rejected.

116.] see Proverbs 10 : 16 (one of many such passages).

As if we knew not thy profession?   120
If thou rely upon thy righteousness,
Be patient and thy riches will increase.
Excess of wealth is cause of covetousness,
And covetousness, O, 'tis a monstrous sin.

BARABAS.

Ay, but theft is worse; tush, take not from me then,   125
For that is theft; and if you rob me thus,
I must be forc'd to steal and compass more.

I KNIGHT.

Grave governors, list not to his exclaims:
Convert his mansion to a nunnery;

Enter Officers.

His house will harbor many holy nuns.   130

FERNEZE.

It shall be so: now, officers, have you done?

I OFFICER.

Ay, my lord, we have seiz'd upon the goods
And wares of Barabas, which being valued
Amount to more than all the wealth in Malta.
And of the other we have seized half.   135

FERNEZE.

Then we'll take order for the residue.

BARABAS.

Well then, my lord, say, are you satisfied?
You have my goods, my money, and my wealth,
My ships, my store, and all that I enjoy'd;
And having all, you can request no more,   140
Unless your unrelenting flinty hearts
Suppress all pity in your stony breasts,
And now shall move you to bereave my life.

129.1.] *Reed; at right-hand margin*   136. S.P. FERNEZE] *Robinson; not in*
after l. 130 Q.   *Q, which continues the speech of the*
                                           Officer.

---

120. *profession*] (1) occupation (2) religion.
128. *exclaims*] outcries, exclamations.
133. *valued*] appraised.
135. *of the other*] from the other Jews.
136. *residue*] i.e., the part seized by Ferneze.

FERNEZE.

No, Barabas, to stain our hands with blood
Is far from us and our profession.   145

BARABAS.

Why, I esteem the injury far less,
To take the lives of miserable men,
Than be the causers of their misery;
You have my wealth, the labor of my life,
The comfort of mine age, my children's hope;   150
And therefore ne'er distinguish of the wrong.

FERNEZE.

Content thee, Barabas; thou hast naught but right.

BARABAS.

Your extreme right does me exceeding wrong:
But take it to you i' th' devil's name.

FERNEZE.

Come, let us in, and gather of these goods   155
The money for this tribute of the Turk.

I KNIGHT.

'Tis necessary that be look'd unto:
For if we break our day, we break the league,
And that will prove but simple policy.

                    Exeunt. [*Manent* Barabas *and the three* Jews.]

BARABAS.

Ay, policy! that's their profession,   160
And not simplicity, as they suggest.
The plagues of Egypt, and the curse of heaven,
Earth's barrenness, and all men's hatred
Inflict upon them, thou great *Primus Motor.*
And here upon my knees, striking the earth,   165

164. *Primus*] *Reed; Primas Q.*

---

145. *profession*] faith.
151. *distinguish of*] "make...subtle distinctions with regard to" (*OED*).
153. *extreme*] harsh.   155. *gather of*] obtain from.
158. *break our day*] fail to keep the time appointed for our payment.
159. *simple policy*] foolish statecraft.
159.1. *Manent*] remain.
160. *policy*] political cunning.
161. *simplicity*] straightforwardness.
164. *Primus Motor*] "the original source of motion" (Bennett)—i.e., God.

I ban their souls to everlasting pains
And extreme tortures of the fiery deep
That thus have dealt with me in my distress.

I JEW.

O, yet be patient, gentle Barabas.

BARABAS.

O, silly brethren, born to see this day!   170
Why stand you thus unmov'd with my laments?
Why weep you not to think upon my wrongs?
Why pine not I, and die in this distress?

I JEW.

Why, Barabas, as hardly can we brook
The cruel handling of ourselves in this: 175
Thou seest they have taken half our goods.

BARABAS.

Why did you yield to their extortion?
You were a multitude, and I but one,
And of me only have they taken all.

I JEW.

Yet, brother Barabas, remember Job.   180

BARABAS.

What tell you me of Job? I wot his wealth
Was written thus: he had seven thousand sheep,
Three thousand camels, and two hundred yoke
Of laboring oxen, and five hundred
She asses; but for every one of those,   185
Had they been valued at indifferent rate,
I had at home, and in mine argosy
And other ships that came from Egypt last,
As much as would have bought his beasts and him,
And yet have kept enough to live upon;   190
So that not he, but I may curse the day,
Thy fatal birthday, forlorn Barabas,
And henceforth wish for an eternal night,
That clouds of darkness may enclose my flesh,

---

166. *ban*] curse.   174. *as hardly*] with as much difficulty.
181. *wot*] know.   182–185.] see Job 1 : 3.
186. *indifferent rate*] fair estimate of worth.
188. *last*] most recently.   191–192.] see Job 3 : 1–9.

And hide these extreme sorrows from mine eyes: 195
For only I have toil'd to inherit here
The months of vanity and loss of time,
And painful nights have been appointed me.

2 JEW.

Good Barabas, be patient.

BARABAS.   Ay, ay;

Pray leave me in my patience. You that   200
Were ne'er possess'd of wealth, are pleas'd with want.
But give him liberty at least to mourn,
That in a field amidst his enemies
Doth see his soldiers slain, himself disarm'd,
And knows no means of his recovery: 205
Ay, let me sorrow for this sudden chance;
'Tis in the trouble of my spirit I speak.
Great injuries are not so soon forgot.

I JEW.

Come, let us leave him in his ireful mood;
Our words will but increase his ecstasy.   210

2 JEW.

On then; but trust me 'tis a misery
To see a man in such affliction.
Farewell, Barabas.   *Exeunt.* [*Manet* Barabas.]

BARABAS.   Ay, fare you well.

See the simplicity of these base slaves,
Who, for the villains have no wit themselves,   215
Think me to be a senseless lump of clay
That will with every water wash to dirt:
No, Barabas is born to better chance,
And fram'd of finer mold than common men,
That measure naught but by the present time.   220
A reaching thought will search his deepest wits,
And cast with cunning for the time to come:

196.] for I have toiled to inherit here only.   197–198.] see Job 7 : 3.
205. *of*] for.   206. *sudden chance*] unexpected misfortune.
207.] see Job 7 : 11.   210. *ecstasy*] frenzy.
214. *simplicity*] folly.   215. *for*] because.
215. *wit*] intelligence.   218. *chance*] fortune.
221. *reaching thought*] ambitious thinker (Brooke 2).
222. *cast*] contrive.

For evils are apt to happen every day—
But whither wends my beauteous Abigail?

Enter Abigail, *the Jew's daughter.*

O, what has made my lovely daughter sad?   225
What? woman, moan not for a little loss:
Thy father has enough in store for thee.

ABIGAIL.
Not for myself, but aged Barabas:
Father, for thee lamenteth Abigail.
But I will learn to leave these fruitless tears,   230
And, urg'd thereto with my afflictions,
With fierce exclaims run to the senate-house,
And in the senate reprehend them all,
And rent their hearts with tearing of my hair,
Till they reduce the wrongs done to my father.   235

BARABAS.
No, Abigail, things past recovery
Are hardly cur'd with exclamations.
Be silent, daughter; sufferance breeds ease,
And time may yield us an occasion
Which on the sudden cannot serve the turn.   240
Besides, my girl, think me not all so fond
As negligently to forgo so much
Without provision for thyself and me.
Ten thousand portagues, besides great pearls,
Rich, costly jewels, and stones infinite,   245
Fearing the worst of this before it fell,
I closely hid.

ABIGAIL.   Where, father?

BARABAS.   In my house, my girl.

---

224. *Abigail*] the name of one of King David's wives; see 1 Samuel 25 : 42.
231. *urg'd*] incited.   231. *with*] by.
234. *rent*] rend, tear.   235. *reduce*] redress.
238. *sufferance*] patience.   240. *Which*] has *time* for its antecedent.
240. *on the sudden*] at the moment.
240. *serve the turn*] satisfy the need.
241. *fond*] foolish.   242. *forgo*] lose.
244. *portagues*] Portuguese gold coins, worth £3 10s. to £4 10s. (Nares).
247. *closely*] secretly.

ABIGAIL.

Then shall they ne'er be seen of Barabas:
For they have seiz'd upon thy house and wares.

BARABAS.

But they will give me leave once more, I trow,   250
To go into my house.

ABIGAIL.   That may they not:
For there I left the governor placing nuns,
Displacing me; and of thy house they mean
To make a nunnery, where none but their own sect
Must enter in, men generally barr'd.   255

BARABAS.

My gold, my gold, and all my wealth is gone!
You partial heavens, have I deserv'd this plague?
What, will you thus oppose me, luckless stars,
To make me desperate in my poverty?
And knowing me impatient in distress   260
Think me so mad as I will hang myself,
That I may vanish o'er the earth in air,
And leave no memory that e'er I was?
No! I will live; nor loathe I this my life;
And since you leave me in the ocean thus   265
To sink or swim, and put me to my shifts,
I'll rouse my senses, and awake myself.
Daughter, I have it: thou perceiv'st the plight
Wherein these Christians have oppressed me:
Be rul'd by me, for in extremity   270
We ought to make bar of no policy.

ABIGAIL.

Father, whate'er it be, to injure them
That have so manifestly wronged us,
What will not Abigail attempt?

BARABAS.   Why, so;
Then thus: thou told'st me they have turn'd my house   275
Into a nunnery, and some nuns are there.

---

250. *I trow*] I daresay.   253. *they*] i.e., the nuns.
254. *sect*] sex.   255. *generally*] without exception.
258. *luckless*] foreboding evil.
266. *put me to my shifts*] leave me in extremity.

ABIGAIL.

I did.

BARABAS.   Then, Abigail, there must my girl

Entreat the Abbess to be entertain'd.

ABIGAIL.

How, as a nun?

BARABAS.   Ay, daughter, for religion

Hides many mischiefs from suspicion.   280

ABIGAIL.

Ay, but, father, they will suspect me there.

BARABAS.

Let 'em suspect, but be thou so precise

As they may think it done of holiness.

Entreat 'em fair, and give them friendly speech,

And seem to them as if thy sins were great,   285

Till thou hast gotten to be entertain'd.

ABIGAIL.

Thus, father, shall I much dissemble.

BARABAS.   Tush!

As good dissemble that thou never mean'st,

As first mean truth, and then dissemble it.

A counterfeit profession is better   290

Than unseen hypocrisy.

ABIGAIL.   Well, father,

Say I be entertain'd; what then shall follow?

BARABAS.

This shall follow then:

There have I hid close underneath the plank

That runs along the upper-chamber floor,   295

The gold and jewels which I kept for thee.

But here they come; be cunning, Abigail.

ABIGAIL.

Then, father, go with me.

---

278. *entertain'd*] taken into service.

282. *precise*] scrupulous in religious observance; puritanical.

284. *fair*] in a proper manner.

286.] "Till you have got yourself received" (Bennett).

290. *counterfeit*] pretended.

290. *profession*] promise made on entering a religious order.

291. *unseen*] hidden, undetected.

BARABAS.   No, Abigail, in this
    It is not necessary I be seen,
    For I will seem offended with thee for 't.   300
    Be close, my girl, for this must fetch my gold.

Enter three Friars [*including* Jacomo *and* Barnardine] *and two Nuns*
[*one an* Abbess].

FRIAR JACOMO.
    Sisters, we now are almost at the new-made nunnery.
ABBESS.
    The better; for we love not to be seen:
    'Tis thirty winters long since some of us
    Did stray so far amongst the multitude.   305
FRIAR JACOMO.
    But, madam, this house and waters of this new-made
    nunnery will much delight you.
ABBESS.
    It may be so; but who comes here?
ABIGAIL.
    Grave Abbess, and you, happy virgins' guide,
    Pity the state of a distressed maid.   310
ABBESS.
    What art thou, daughter?
ABIGAIL.
    The hopeless daughter of a hapless Jew,
    The Jew of Malta, wretched Barabas,
    Sometimes the owner of a goodly house,
    Which they have now turn'd to a nunnery.   315
ABBESS.
    Well, daughter, say, what is thy suit with us?
ABIGAIL.
    Fearing the afflictions which my father feels
    Proceed from sin, or want of faith in us,
    I'd pass away my life in penitence,

303. S.P. ABBESS] *Dyce 1; 1 Nun. Q*.   308. S.P. ABBESS] *Dyce 1; Nun. Q*.

299.] "i.e. It is necessary I be not seen" (Bennett).
301. *close*] secretive.
309. *guide*] the friars, confessors to the nuns.
314. *Sometimes*] formerly.

And be a novice in your nunnery,   320
To make atonement for my laboring soul.

FRIAR JACOMO.

No doubt, brother, but this proceedeth of the spirit.

FRIAR BARNARDINE.

Ay, and of a moving spirit too, brother; but come,
Let us entreat she may be entertain'd.

ABBESS.

Well, daughter, we admit you for a nun.   325

ABIGAIL.

First let me as a novice learn to frame
My solitary life to your strait laws,
And let me lodge where I was wont to lie;
I do not doubt, by your divine precepts
And mine own industry, but to profit much.   330

BARABAS (aside).

As much, I hope, as all I hid is worth.

ABBESS.

Come, daughter, follow us.

BARABAS.   Why, how now, Abigail?
What mak'st thou amongst these hateful Christians?

FRIAR JACOMO.

Hinder her not, thou man of little faith,
For she has mortified herself.

BARABAS.   How, mortified!   335

FRIAR JACOMO.

And is admitted to the sisterhood.

BARABAS.

Child of perdition, and thy father's shame,
What wilt thou do among these hateful fiends?
I charge thee on my blessing that thou leave
These devils, and their damned heresy.   340

---

321. *laboring*] struggling under emotion.
323. *moving spirit*]? a disposition which excites the passions.
326. *frame*] discipline.
327. *strait*] strict, rigorous.
333. *What mak'st thou*] what are you doing.
335. *mortified herself*] made herself dead to sin and the world by joining a religious order.
337. *perdition*] damnation.   339. *charge*] command.

ABIGAIL.

    Father, give me—

BARABAS.   Nay, back, Abigail.

    (*whispers to her*) And think upon the jewels and the gold;

    The board is marked thus [*makes cross*] that covers it.

    —Away, accursed, from thy father's sight.

FRIAR JACOMO.

    Barabas, although thou art in misbelief,   345

    And wilt not see thine own afflictions,

    Yet let thy daughter be no longer blind.

BARABAS.

    Blind? Friar, I reck not thy persuasions.

    [*aside to* Abigail] The board is marked thus [*makes cross*] that

        covers it.

    —For I had rather die, than see her thus.   350

    Wilt thou forsake me too in my distress,

    Seduced daughter? (*aside to her*) Go, forget not.

    —Becomes it Jews to be so credulous?

    (*aside to her*) Tomorrow early I'll be at the door.

    —No, come not at me, if thou wilt be damn'd.   355

    Forget me, see me not, and so be gone.

    (*aside* [*to her*]) Farewell; remember tomorrow morning.

    —Out, out, thou wretch.   [*Exeunt,* Barabas *separately.*]

                    Enter Mathias.

MATHIAS.

    Who's this? fair Abigail, the rich Jew's daughter,

    Become a nun! Her father's sudden fall   360

    Has humbled her and brought her down to this.

    Tut, she were fitter for a tale of love

    Than to be tired out with orisons;

    And better would she far become a bed,

    Embraced in a friendly lover's arms,   365

    Than rise at midnight to a solemn mass.

342. *whispers to her*] *Robinson; at*   343. *Q*.
right-hand margin opposite ll. 342 and   343. *makes cross*] *Kirschbaum;* † *Q*.

345. *misbelief*] heresy.
348. *reck not*] am unmoved by.
348. *persuasions*] (1) arguments (2) beliefs.
363. *orisons*] prayers.

Enter Lodowick.

LODOWICK.
     Why, how now, Don Mathias, in a dump?

MATHIAS.
     Believe me, noble Lodowick, I have seen
     The strangest sight, in my opinion,
     That ever I beheld.

LODOWICK.   What was 't, I prithee?   370

MATHIAS.
     A fair young maid, scarce fourteen years of age,
     The sweetest flower in Cytherea's field,
     Cropp'd from the pleasures of the fruitful earth,
     And strangely metamorphos'd nun.

LODOWICK.
     But say, what was she?

MATHIAS.   Why, the rich Jew's daughter.   375

LODOWICK.
     What, Barabas, whose goods were lately seiz'd?
     Is she so fair?

MATHIAS.   And matchless beautiful;
     As had you seen her 'twould have mov'd your heart,
     Though countermur'd with walls of brass, to love,
     Or at the least to pity.   380

LODOWICK.
     And if she be so fair as you report,
     'Twere time well spent to go and visit her:
     How say you, shall we?

MATHIAS.
     I must and will, sir; there's no remedy.

LODOWICK.
     And so will I too, or it shall go hard.   385

---

379. countermur'd] *conj. Collier, MS*
(*so Bennett*); countermin'd Q.

---

     367. *dump*] state of amazement.   372. *Cytherea*] Venus.
     379. *countermur'd*] "protected by one wall behind another as a reserve
defence" (Bennett).
     385. *or it shall go hard*] "unless overwhelming difficulties prevent"
(Onions).

Farewell, Mathias.

MATHIAS.   Farewell, Lodowick.   *Exeunt* [*severally*].

[II.i]   *Enter* Barabas *with a light*.

BARABAS.
Thus like the sad presaging raven that tolls
The sick man's passport in her hollow beak,
And in the shadow of the silent night
Doth shake contagion from her sable wings,
Vex'd and tormented runs poor Barabas   5
With fatal curses towards these Christians.
The incertain pleasures of swift-footed time
Have ta'en their flight, and left me in despair;
And of my former riches rests no more
But bare remembrance, like a soldier's scar,   10
That has no further comfort for his maim.
O, Thou, that with a fiery pillar ledd'st
The sons of Israel through the dismal shades,
Light Abraham's offspring, and direct the hand
Of Abigail this night; or let the day   15
Turn to eternal darkness after this:
No sleep can fasten on my watchful eyes,
Nor quiet enter my distemper'd thoughts,
Till I have answer of my Abigail.

Enter Abigail *above*.

ABIGAIL.
Now have I happily espied a time   20
To search the plank my father did appoint;
And here, behold, unseen, where I have found
The gold, the pearls, and jewels which he hid.

---

1. *raven*] believed by the Elizabethans to be an omen of ill.
2. *passport*] i.e., to the other world.   9. *rests*] remains.
11.] i.e., only the scar (small consolation) is left as recompense for the wound he suffered.
11. *comfort*] relief.   12–13.] see Exodus 13 : 21.
17. *watchful*] wakeful, sleepless.
18. *distemper'd*] troubled.   21. *appoint*] point out.

BARABAS.

    Now I remember those old women's words,
    Who in my wealth would tell me winter's tales,   25
    And speak of spirits and ghosts that glide by night
    About the place where treasure hath been hid;
    And now methinks that I am one of those:
    For whilst I live, here lives my soul's sole hope,
    And when I die, here shall my spirit walk.   30

ABIGAIL.

    Now that my father's fortune were so good
    As but to be about this happy place—
    'Tis not so happy; yet when we parted last,
    He said he would attend me in the morn.
    Then, gentle sleep, where'er his body rests,   35
    Give charge to Morpheus that he may dream
    A golden dream, and of the sudden walk,
    Come and receive the treasure I have found.

BARABAS.

    Bien para todos mi ganada no es:
    As good go on, as sit so sadly thus.   40
    But stay! what star shines yonder in the east?
    The lodestar of my life, if Abigail.
    Who's there?

ABIGAIL.   Who's that?

BARABAS.   Peace, Abigail, 'tis I.

ABIGAIL.

    Then, father, here receive thy happiness.

BARABAS.

    Hast thou 't?   45

ABIGAIL.

    Here.   (*Throws down bags.*)   Hast thou 't?

39.] *this edn.; Birn para todos, my*   46. S.D.] *Dyce 1; at right-hand*
ganada no er Q.   *margin after l. 45* Q.

  25. *wealth*] prosperity.
  25. *winter's tales*] idle stories, fairy tales.
  34. *attend*] expect; wait for.
  36. *Morpheus*] Greek god of dreams.
  37. *walk*] obsolete form of *wake* (*OED*).
  39.] what's good for everybody else is of no benefit to me.
  42. *lodestar*] polestar, hence, guiding star.

There's more, and more, and more.

BARABAS.   O, my girl,

My gold, my fortune, my felicity;
Strength to my soul, death to mine enemy;
Welcome, the first beginner of my bliss!   50
O, Abigail, that I had thee here too,
Then my desires were fully satisfied;
But I will practice thy enlargement thence.
O girl, O gold, O beauty, O my bliss!   *Hugs his bags.*

ABIGAIL.

Father, it draweth towards midnight now,   55
And 'bout this time the nuns begin to wake;
To shun suspicion, therefore, let us part.

BARABAS.

Farewell, my joy, and by my fingers take
A kiss from him that sends it from his soul.

                             [Exit Abigail *above.]*

Now, Phoebus, ope the eyelids of the day,   60
And, for the raven, wake the morning lark,
That I may hover with her in the air,
Singing o'er these, as she does o'er her young.
Hermoso placer de los dineros.   *Exit.*

[II.ii]

    Enter Ferneze, Martin del Bosco, *the* Knights [, *and Officers*].

FERNEZE.

Now, captain, tell us whither thou art bound,
Whence is thy ship that anchors in our road,
And why thou cam'st ashore without our leave?

DEL BOSCO.

Governor of Malta, hither am I bound;

51. Abigail] *this edn.; Aigal, Abigal*
Q.

64. *Hermoso...dineros] Dyce 1; Hermoso Piarer, de les Denirch. Q.*
64. *Exit] Dyce 1; Exeunt. Q.*

53. *practice*] "devise means to bring about" (*OED*).
53. *enlargement*] release from confinement.
60. *Phoebus*] Apollo, as god of the sun.
61. *for*] instead of.
61. *raven . . . lark*] associated with night and day, respectively.
64.] beautiful pleasure of money.

My ship, *The Flying Dragon*, is of Spain,   5
And so am I; del Bosco is my name,
Vice-admiral unto the Catholic king.

1 KNIGHT.

'Tis true, my lord; therefore entreat him well.

DEL BOSCO.

Our fraught is Grecians, Turks, and Afric Moors.
For late upon the coast of Corsica,   10
Because we vail'd not to the Turkish fleet,
Their creeping galleys had us in the chase;
But suddenly the wind began to rise,
And then we luff'd and tack'd, and fought at ease.
Some have we fir'd, and many have we sunk,   15
But one amongst the rest became our prize:
The captain's slain, the rest remain our slaves,
Of whom we would make sale in Malta here.

FERNEZE.

Martin del Bosco, I have heard of thee;
Welcome to Malta, and to all of us.   20
But to admit a sale of these thy Turks
We may not, nay, we dare not give consent,
By reason of a tributary league.

1 KNIGHT.

Del Bosco, as thou lovest and honor'st us,
Persuade our governor against the Turk.   25
This truce we have is but in hope of gold,
And with that sum he craves might we wage war.

DEL BOSCO.

Will Knights of Malta be in league with Turks,
And buy it basely, too, for sums of gold?

11. Turkish] *Scott; Spanish Q.*   14. luff'd and tack'd] *Dyce 1;* left,
                                          and tooke *Q.*

---

8. *entreat*] deal with, treat.
9. *fraught*] cargo.   10. *late*] recently.
11. *vail'd not*] did not lower sails in acknowledgment of inferiority (*OED*).
14. *luff'd and tack'd*] sailed close to the wind and obliquely against it.
15. *fir'd*] set on fire.
23. *tributary league*] "an alliance on terms of monetary payments"
(Bennett).
29. *it*] i.c., alliance.

My lord, remember that, to Europe's shame,   30
The Christian isle of Rhodes, from whence you came,
Was lately lost, and you were stated here
To be at deadly enmity with Turks.

FERNEZE.

Captain, we know it, but our force is small.

DEL BOSCO.

What is the sum that Calymath requires?   35

FERNEZE.

A hundred thousand crowns.

DEL BOSCO.

My lord and king hath title to this isle,
And he means quickly to expel you hence;
Therefore be rul'd by me, and keep the gold.
I'll write unto his Majesty for aid   40
And not depart until I see you free.

FERNEZE.

On this condition shall thy Turks be sold.
Go, officers, and set them straight in show.   [*Exeunt Officers.*]
Bosco, thou shalt be Malta's general;
We and our warlike knights will follow thee   45
Against these barbarous misbelieving Turks.

DEL BOSCO.

So shall you imitate those you succeed:
For when their hideous force environ'd Rhodes,
Small though the number was that kept the town,
They fought it out, and not a man surviv'd   50
To bring the hapless news to Christendom.

FERNEZE.

So will we fight it out; come, let's away.
Proud, daring Calymath, instead of gold,
We'll send thee bullets wrapp'd in smoke and fire;
Claim tribute where thou wilt, we are resolv'd;   55
Honor is bought with blood and not with gold.   *Exeunt.*

54. thee] *Reed;* the *Q*.

---

32. *stated*] placed.
43. *set them straight in show*] put them on display immediately.
46. *misbelieving*] heretical.
51. *hapless*] unfortunate.

[II.iii]   *Enter* Officers *with* [Ithamore *and other*] Slaves.

1 OFFICER.

   This is the marketplace; here let 'em stand:
   Fear not their sale, for they'll be quickly bought.

2 OFFICER.

   Every one's price is written on his back,
   And so much must they yield or not be sold.

                    Enter Barabas.

1 OFFICER.

   Here comes the Jew; had not his goods been seiz'd,   5
   He'd give us present money for them all.

BARABAS.

   In spite of these swine-eating Christians
   (Unchosen nation, never circumcis'd,
   Such as, poor villains, were ne'er thought upon
   Till Titus and Vespasian conquer'd us),   10
   Am I become as wealthy as I was.
   They hop'd my daughter would ha' been a nun,
   But she's at home, and I have bought a house
   As great and fair as is the governor's;
   And there in spite of Malta will I dwell,   15
   Having Ferneze's hand, whose heart I'll have;
   Ay, and his son's, too, or it shall go hard.
   I am not of the Tribe of Levi, I,
   That can so soon forget an injury.
   We Jews can fawn like spaniels when we please,   20
   And when we grin, we bite; yet are our looks
   As innocent and harmless as a lamb's.
   I learn'd in Florence how to kiss my hand,

4.1.] *Ent. Bar. at right-hand margin*   6.] *following   this   line   Q   has   a*
after l. 4 Q.   *centered S.D.: Enter Barabas.*

---

   6. *present money*] ready cash.   9. *villains*] low-born rustics.
   10.] Jerusalem fell September 8, A.D. 70, following a campaign led first
by Vespasian, who was declared Emperor of Rome in 69, and then by his
son Titus (Emperor in 79).
   16. *Having Ferneze's hand*] with the written agreement of Ferneze.
   18. *Tribe of Levi*] the priestly tribe, holding jurisdiction over the cities of
refuge, where slayers were free from blood vengeance; see Joshua 21.
   23. *Florence*] the home of Machiavelli.

Heave up my shoulders when they call me dog,
And duck as low as any barefoot friar,   25
Hoping to see them starve upon a stall,
Or else be gather'd for in our synagogue,
That when the offering basin comes to me,
Even for charity I may spit into 't.
Here comes Don Lodowick, the governor's son,   30
One that I love for his good father's sake.

Enter Lodowick.

LODOWICK.

I hear the wealthy Jew walked this way;
I'll seek him out, and so insinuate
That I may have a sight of Abigail;
For Don Mathias tells me she is fair.   35

BARABAS [*aside*].

Now will I show myself to have more of the serpent than
the dove; that is, more knave than fool.

LODOWICK.

Yond walks the Jew; now for fair Abigail.

BARABAS [*aside*].

Ay, ay; no doubt but she's at your command.

LODOWICK.

Barabas, thou know'st I am the governor's son.   40

BARABAS.

I would you were his father too, sir; that's all the harm I
wish you. [*aside*] The slave looks like a hog's cheek new
sing'd.

LODOWICK.

Whither walk'st thou, Barabas?

BARABAS.

No further: 'tis a custom held with us,   45
That when we speak with Gentiles like to you,

---

25. *duck*] bow humbly.

26. *stall*] bench in front of Elizabethan shops where wares were displayed;
the impoverished sometimes slept on the stalls at night.

27. *be gather'd*] a collection be taken.

33. *insinuate*] ingratiate myself.   36–37.] see Matthew 10 : 16.

42–43. *The slave...sing'd*] i.e., Don Lodowick affectedly goes clean
shaven.

We turn into the air to purge ourselves:
For unto us the promise doth belong.

LODOWICK.

Well, Barabas, canst help me to a diamond?

BARABAS.

O, sir, your father had my diamonds.   50
Yet I have one left that will serve your turn:
(*aside*) I mean my daughter; but ere he shall have her,
I'll sacrifice her on a pile of wood.
I ha' the poison of the city for him,
And the white leprosy.   55

LODOWICK.

What sparkle does it give without a foil?

BARABAS.

The diamond that I talk of ne'er was foil'd;
[*aside*] But when he touches it, it will be foil'd.
[*to him*] Lord Lodowick, it sparkles bright and fair.

LODOWICK.

Is it square or pointed? pray let me know.   60

BARABAS.

Pointed it is, good sir; (*aside*) but not for you.

LODOWICK.

I like it much the better.

BARABAS.   So do I, too.

LODOWICK.

How shows it by night?

52. *aside*] *Dyce   1;   at   right-hand*
margin after l. 53 Q.

---

47. *turn*] stroll.   47. *purge ourselves*] cleanse ourselves of defilement.
48.] see, e.g., Exodus 6 : 1–13.
54. *poison of the city*] not satisfactorily explained.
55. *white leprosy*] the most unpleasant stage of the disease, when shining
white scales form on the skin.
56. *foil*] thin metal leaf placed under a precious stone to increase its
brilliancy; here, with a pun on the proper "setting" for Abigail's beauty.
57. *foil'd*] displayed with a foil; here, as a wealthy man's daughter could
be presented.
58. *foil'd*] defiled, especially (of a woman's chastity), violated.
61. *Pointed*] with a pun on *appointed*.

BARABAS.　　　　　　　　　Outshines Cynthia's rays:
　(*aside*) You'll like it better far a' nights than days.
LODOWICK.
　And what's the price?
BARABAS.　　　　　　　　　[*aside*] Your life, and if you have it.　65
　[*to him*] O, my lord,
　We will not jar about the price; come to my house,
　And I will give 't your honor—(*aside*) with a vengeance.
LODOWICK.
　No, Barabas, I will deserve it first.
BARABAS.
　Good sir,　　　　　　　　　　　　　　　　　　　70
　Your father has deserv'd it at my hands,
　Who, of mere charity and Christian ruth,
　To bring me to religious purity,
　And, as it were, in catechizing sort,
　To make me mindful of my mortal sins,　　　　　75
　Against my will, and whether I would or no,
　Seiz'd all I had, and thrust me out a' doors,
　And made my house a place for nuns most chaste.
LODOWICK.
　No doubt your soul shall reap the fruit of it.
BARABAS.
　Ay, but, my lord, the harvest is far off;　　　　80
　And yet I know the prayers of those nuns
　And holy friars, having money for their pains,
　Are wondrous; (*aside*) and indeed do no man good.
　[*to him*] And seeing they are not idle, but still doing,
　'Tis likely they in time may reap some fruit;　85
　I mean in fullness of perfection.
LODOWICK.
　Good Barabas, glance not at our holy nuns.

---

　63. *Cynthia*] the moon (personified as Artemis, goddess of Greek mythology).
　64.] the bawdy suggestion is obvious.　　67. *jar*] quarrel.
　72. *ruth*] compassion (with a possible pun on the sense *mischief*).
　74. *in catechizing sort*] in the fashion of religious instruction.
　84. *doing*] copulating.
　86. *fullness of perfection*] (1) state of perfect Christian holiness (2) end of the period of gestation.
　87. *glance*] refer satirically.

BARABAS.

No, but I do it through a burning zeal,
(*aside*) Hoping ere long to set the house afire;
For though they do a while increase and multiply,   90
I'll have a saying to that nunnery.
[*to him*] As for the diamond, sir, I told you of,
Come home, and there's no price shall make us part,
Even for your honorable father's sake.
(*aside*) It shall go hard but I will see your death.   95
[*to him*] But now I must be gone to buy a slave.

LODOWICK.

And, Barabas, I'll bear thee company.

BARABAS.

Come, then; here's the marketplace.
What's the price of this slave? Two hundred crowns?
Do the Turk weigh so much?

1 OFFICER.   Sir, that's his price.   100

BARABAS.

What, can he steal that you demand so much?
Belike he has some new trick for a purse;
And if he has, he is worth three hundred plates,
So that, being bought, the town seal might be got
To keep him for his lifetime from the gallows.   105
The sessions day is critical to thieves,
And few or none 'scape but by being purg'd.

89. *aside*] *Oxberry 1; at right-hand
margin after l. 90 Q*.

---

88. *burning zeal*] ardent devotion (with a pun made obvious by the next line).

91. *have a saying to*] "have something to say to" (*OED*).

95.] unless overwhelming difficulties prevent it, I'll see to it that you die.

99. *crowns*] coins with the imprint of a crown.

102. *trick for a purse*] means of stealing a purse.

103–107.] "If he has a new way of purse-stealing, he is worth three hundred plates, provided that a perpetual pardon or charter with the town-seal upon it can be got to keep him from the gallows, since the Sessions-days are crucial to thieves, and few or none escape except they are purged of their offences" (Bennett).

103. *plates*] silver coins, especially a Spanish one: the eighth part of a piastre.

107. *purg'd*] (1) cleared of guilt (2) got rid of (by hanging).

LODOWICK.

Ratest thou this Moor but at two hundred plates?

I OFFICER.

No more, my lord.

BARABAS.

Why should this Turk be dearer than that Moor?   110

I OFFICER.

Because he is young and has more qualities.

BARABAS.

What, hast the philosopher's stone? And thou hast, break
my head with it; I'll forgive thee.

I SLAVE.

No, sir; I can cut and shave.

BARABAS.

Let me see, sirrah; are you not an old shaver?   115

I SLAVE.

Alas, sir, I am a very youth.

BARABAS.

A youth? I'll buy you and marry you to Lady Vanity, if
you do well.

I SLAVE.

I will serve you, sir.

BARABAS.

Some wicked trick or other. It may be under color of 120
shaving thou 'lt cut my throat for my goods. Tell me, hast
thou thy health well?

I SLAVE.

Ay, passing well.

114. S.P. I SLAVE] *Reed; speech   123, Q.*
assigned to Itha., as in ll. 116, 119,

---

108. *Ratest thou*] do you price.

111. *qualities*] accomplishments.

112. *philosopher's stone*] the substance sought by alchemists for the
purpose of turning other metals into gold.

112. *And*] if.   115. *old shaver*] joker, prankster.

117. *Lady Vanity*] a composite name for the personified sirens of the old
morality plays (Spivack).

119. *serve*] be a servant; in the next line, Barabas puns on the meaning
play (a trick).

123. *passing*] quite.

BARABAS.

So much the worse; I must have one that's sickly, and be
but for sparing victuals; 'tis not a stone of beef a day will 125
maintain you in these chops. Let me see one that's somewhat leaner.

I OFFICER.

Here's a leaner. How like you him?

BARABAS.

Where was thou born?

ITHAMORE.

In Thrace; brought up in Arabia.   130

BARABAS.

So much the better; thou art for my turn.
An hundred crowns? I'll have him; there's the coin.

I OFFICER.

Then mark him, sir, and take him hence.

BARABAS [aside].

Ay, mark him, you were best; for this is he
That by my help shall do much villainy.   135
—My lord, farewell. [to Ithamore] Come, sirrah, you are
    mine.
[to Lodowick] As for the diamond, it shall be yours.
I pray, sir, be no stranger at my house;
All that I have shall be at your command.

Enter Mathias [*and his*] *Mother* [, Katherine].

MATHIAS [aside].

What makes the Jew and Lodowick so private?   140
I fear me 'tis about fair Abigail.

BARABAS.

Yonder comes Don Mathias; let us stay.
He loves my daughter, and she holds him dear,

139.1.] *Reed* (*subs.*); *Enter Mathias,   prefixes.*
Mater Q, which reads Mater in speech

---

125. *stone*] a measure of weight, usually fourteen pounds.
126. *in these chops*] with such fat cheeks.
130. *Thrace*] a division of Greece.
131. *for my turn*] suitable for my purposes.
133. *mark him*] put your mark on him.
134. *mark him*] note him well.   142. *stay*] stop (our conversation).

But I have sworn to frustrate both their hopes,
And be reveng'd upon the—[*aside*] governor.   145

                                        [*Exit* Lodowick.]

KATHERINE.

This Moor is comeliest, is he not? Speak, son.

MATHIAS.

No, this is the better, mother; view this well.

BARABAS [*aside to* Mathias].

Seem not to know me here before your mother,
Lest she mistrust the match that is in hand.
When you have brought her home, come to my house;   150
Think of me as thy father; son, farewell.

MATHIAS [*aside to* Barabas].

But wherefore talk'd Don Lodowick with you?

BARABAS [*aside to him*].

Tush, man, we talk'd of diamonds, not of Abigail.

KATHERINE.

Tell me, Mathias, is not that the Jew?

BARABAS.

As for the comment on the Maccabees,   155
I have it, sir, and 'tis at your command.

MATHIAS.

Yes, madam, and my talk with him was but
About the borrowing of a book or two.

KATHERINE.

Converse not with him; he is cast off from heaven.
Thou hast thy crowns, fellow. Come, let's away.   160

MATHIAS.

Sirrah Jew, remember the book.

BARABAS.

Marry, will I, sir.   *Exeunt* [Mathias, Katherine, *and* Slave].

I OFFICER.

Come, I have made a reasonable market; let's away.

                                [*Exeunt* Officers *with* Slaves.]

---

157. but] *conj. Dyce 1; not in* Q.   162. S.D. *Exeunt*] *Penley; after l. 160*
                                           Q.

---

149. *mistrust*] suspect.   150. *brought*] escorted.
155. *comment on the Maccabees*] commentary on the last two books of the
Apocrypha.

BARABAS.

　Now let me know thy name, and therewithal
　Thy birth, condition, and profession.   165

ITHAMORE.

　Faith, sir, my birth is but mean, my name's Ithamore, my
　profession what you please.

BARABAS.

　Hast thou no trade? Then listen to my words,
　And I will teach thee that shall stick by thee.
　First, be thou void of these affections: 170
　Compassion, love, vain hope, and heartless fear;
　Be mov'd at nothing, see thou pity none,
　But to thyself smile when the Christians moan.

ITHAMORE.

　O brave, master; I worship your nose for this.

BARABAS.

　As for myself, I walk abroad a' nights   175
　And kill sick people groaning under walls;
　Sometimes I go about and poison wells;
　And now and then, to cherish Christian thieves,
　I am content to lose some of my crowns,
　That I may, walking in my gallery,   180
　See 'em go pinion'd along by my door.
　Being young, I studied physic, and began
　To practice first upon the Italian;
　There I enrich'd the priests with burials,
　And always kept the sexton's arms in ure   185
　With digging graves and ringing dead men's knells.
　And after that was I an engineer,
　And in the wars 'twixt France and Germany,
　Under pretense of helping Charles the Fifth,

169. teach thee] *Reed;* teach *Q.*

---

166. *mean*] of low degree.
166. *Ithamore*] another biblical name; see Numbers 3:2.
170. *affections*] emotions.　　171. *heartless*] lacking in courage.
174. *brave*] wonderful, "terrific."　　178. *cherish*] encourage.
180. *gallery*] balcony.　　181. *pinion'd*] shackled.
182. *physic*] medicine.　　185. *ure*] practice.
187. *engineer*] constructor of military engines.
189. *Charles the Fifth*] 1500–1558, Holy Roman Emperor 1530.

Slew friend and enemy with my stratagems.   190
Then after that was I an usurer,
And with extorting, cozening, forfeiting,
And tricks belonging unto brokery,
I fill'd the jails with bankrouts in a year,
And with young orphans planted hospitals,   195
And every moon made some or other mad,
And now and then one hang himself for grief,
Pinning upon his breast a long great scroll,
How I with interest tormented him.
But mark how I am bless'd for plaguing them: 200
I have as much coin as will buy the town.
But tell me, now, how hast thou spent thy time?

ITHAMORE.

Faith, master,
In setting Christian villages on fire,
Chaining of eunuchs, binding galley slaves.   205
One time I was an hostler in an inn,
And in the nighttime secretly would I steal
To travelers' chambers, and there cut their throats.
Once at Jerusalem, where the pilgrims kneel'd,
I strowed powder on the marble stones,   210
And therewithal their knees would rankle, so
That I have laugh'd a-good to see the cripples
Go limping home to Christendom on stilts.

BARABAS.

Why, this is something! Make account of me
As of thy fellow; we are villains both.   215
Both circumcised, we hate Christians both.
Be true and secret, thou shalt want no gold.

---

190. *stratagems*] tricks of generalship.
191. *usurer*] moneylender.   192. *cozening*] defrauding.
192. *forfeiting*] exacting fines; confiscating.
193. *brokery*] traffic of a middleman, with implication of dishonesty.
194. *bankrouts*] bankrupts.
195. *planted hospitals*] furnished orphanages.
196. *some or other*] someone or other.   199. *with*] i.e., with demands for.
206. *hostler*] stableman.   211. *rankle*] fester.
212. *a-good*] heartily.   213. *stilts*] crutches.
214–215. *Make account of me/ As of*] esteem me as.

But stand aside; here comes Don Lodowick.

Enter Lodowick.

LODOWICK.

O, Barabas, well met;
Where is the diamond you told me of?   220

BARABAS.

I have it for you, sir; please you walk in with me.
What ho, Abigail! open the door, I say.

Enter Abigail.

ABIGAIL.

In good time, father; here are letters come
From Ormus, and the post stays here within.

BARABAS.

Give me the letters; daughter, do you hear?   225
Entertain Lodowick, the governor's son,
With all the courtesy you can afford,
Provided that you keep your maidenhead.
Use him as if he were a—*(aside)* Philistine.
Dissemble, swear, protest, vow to love him;   230
He is not of the seed of Abraham.
—I am a little busy, sir; pray pardon me.
Abigail, bid him welcome for my sake.

ABIGAIL.

For your sake and his own he's welcome hither.

BARABAS.

Daughter, a word more: [*aside to her*] kiss him, speak him fair, 235
And like a cunning Jew so cast about
That ye be both made sure ere you come out.

ABIGAIL [*aside to* Barabas].

O, father, Don Mathias is my love!

BARABAS [*aside to her*].

I know it; yet I say make love to him.
Do, it is requisite it should be so.   240

---

223. *In good time*] (you have arrived) at the right moment.
224. *Ormus*] famous trading city on the Persian gulf.
224. *post*] messenger.   227. *afford*] manage.
235. *speak him fair*] speak kindly to him.   236. *cast about*] scheme.
237. *made sure*] engaged to be married.

—Nay, on my life, it is my factor's hand.
But go you in; I'll think upon the account.

                         [*Exeunt* Lodowick *and* Abigail.]

The account is made, for Lodowick dies.
My factor sends me word a merchant's fled
That owes me for a hundred tun of wine;   245
I weigh it thus much [*snaps his fingers*]: I have wealth enough.
For now by this has he kiss'd Abigail,
And she vows love to him, and he to her.
As sure as heaven rain'd manna for the Jews,
So sure shall he and Don Mathias die.   250
His father was my chiefest enemy.

                Enter Mathias.

Whither goes Don Mathias? Stay a while.

MATHIAS.

Whither but to my fair love Abigail?

BARABAS.

Thou know'st, and heaven can witness it is true,
That I intend my daughter shall be thine.   255

MATHIAS.

Ay, Barabas, or else thou wrong'st me much.

BARABAS.

O, heaven forbid I should have such a thought.
Pardon me though I weep; the governor's son
Will, whether I will or no, have Abigail:
He sends her letters, bracelets, jewels, rings.   260

MATHIAS.

Does she receive them?

BARABAS.

She? no, Mathias, no, but sends them back,
And when he comes, she locks herself up fast;
Yet through the keyhole will he talk to her,

251.1.] *Dyce 1; after l. 252 Q.*

---

241. *factor*] agent.
242. *think upon the account*] consider the financial statement.
243. *account*] reckoning (of responsibility for conduct).
245. *tun*] barrel(s).   249.] see Exodus 16 : 13–15.
251. *was*] i.e., "in the late proceedings" (Spencer).

While she runs to the window, looking out   265
When you should come and hale him from the door.

MATHIAS.

O, treacherous Lodowick!

BARABAS.

Even now, as I came home, he slipp'd me in,
And I am sure he is with Abigail.

MATHIAS.

I'll rouse him thence.   270

BARABAS.

Not for all Malta; therefore sheathe your sword.
If you love me, no quarrels in my house;
But steal you in, and seem to see him not.
I'll give him such a warning ere he goes
As he shall have small hopes of Abigail.   275
Away, for here they come.

Enter Lodowick [*and*] Abigail.

MATHIAS.

What, hand in hand! I cannot suffer this.

BARABAS.

Mathias, as thou lov'st me, not a word.

MATHIAS.

Well, let it pass; another time shall serve.   *Exit.*

LODOWICK.

Barabas, is not that the widow's son?   280

BARABAS.

Ay, and take heed, for he hath sworn your death.

LODOWICK.

My death? what, is the base-born peasant mad?

BARABAS.

No, no; but happily he stands in fear
Of that which you, I think, ne'er dream upon:
My daughter here, a paltry, silly girl.   285

---

266. *hale*] drag.
268. *slipp'd me in*] i.e., slipped past me.
270. *rouse*] "cause (game) to rise or issue from cover or lair" (*OED*)—
hence contemptuous.
282. *peasant*] low fellow; rascal.   285. *silly*] insignificant.

LODOWICK.

Why, loves she Don Mathias?

BARABAS.

Doth she not with her smiling answer you?

ABIGAIL [aside].

He has my heart; I smile against my will.

LODOWICK.

Barabas, thou know'st I have lov'd thy daughter long.

BARABAS.

And so has she done you, even from a child.   290

LODOWICK.

And now I can no longer hold my mind.

BARABAS.

Nor I the affection that I bear to you.

LODOWICK.

This is thy diamond; tell me, shall I have it?

BARABAS.

Win it, and wear it; it is yet unsoil'd.
O, but I know your lordship would disdain   295
To marry with the daughter of a Jew;
And yet I'll give her many a golden cross,
With Christian posies round about the ring.

LODOWICK.

'Tis not thy wealth, but her that I esteem,
Yet crave I thy consent.   300

BARABAS.

And mine you have; yet let me talk to her.
(aside [to Abigail]) This offspring of Cain, this Jebusite,
That never tasted of the Passover,
Nor e'er shall see the land of Canaan,
Nor our Messias that is yet to come,   305

302. aside] Oxberry 1; at right-hand
margin after l. 305, Q.

---

291. hold my mind] i.e., refrain from speaking.
297. cross] coin with a cross stamped on one side.
298. posies] mottoes; here, inscriptions on the coins.
298. ring] edge of a coin.
302. Jebusite] member of a tribe of Canaan, defeated by the forces of
King David; see 1 Chronicles 11 : 4–9.

This gentle maggot Lodowick, I mean,
Must be deluded: let him have thy hand,
But keep thy heart till Don Mathias comes.

ABIGAIL [*aside to* Barabas].

What, shall I be betroth'd to Lodowick?

BARABAS [*aside to her*].

It's no sin to deceive a Christian,   310
For they themselves hold it a principle
Faith is not to be held with heretics;
But all are heretics that are not Jews;
This follows well, and therefore, daughter, fear not.
—I have entreated her, and she will grant.   315

LODOWICK.

Then, gentle Abigail, plight thy faith to me.

ABIGAIL.

I cannot choose, seeing my father bids:
Nothing but death shall part my love and me.

LODOWICK.

Now have I that for which my soul hath long'd.

BARABAS (*aside*).

So have not I, but yet I hope I shall.   320

ABIGAIL [*aside*].

O, wretched Abigail, what hast thee done?

LODOWICK.

Why on the sudden is your color chang'd?

ABIGAIL.

I know not; but farewell, I must be gone.

BARABAS.

Stay her, but let her not speak one word more.

LODOWICK.

Mute o' the sudden; here's a sudden change.   325

BARABAS.

O, muse not at it; 'tis the Hebrews' guise
That maidens new-betroth'd should weep a while.

---

306. *gentle*] with the common pun on *gentile*; the substantive *gentle* is,
as well, a word for *maggot*.

316. *plight thy faith to me*] give thy formal promise to marry me (the
trothplight, a binding vow in Elizabethan times).

324. *Stay*] stop.   326. *guise*] usual manner, custom.

Trouble her not, sweet Lodowick; depart;
She is thy wife, and thou shalt be mine heir.

LODOWICK.

O, is 't the custom? Then I am resolv'd;   330
But rather let the brightsome heavens be dim,
And nature's beauty choke with stifling clouds,
Than my fair Abigail should frown on me.
There comes the villain; now I'll be reveng'd.

Enter Mathias.

BARABAS.

Be quiet, Lodowick; it is enough   335
That I have made thee sure to Abigail.

LODOWICK.

Well, let him go.   *Exit.*

BARABAS.

Well, but for me, as you went in at doors
You had been stabb'd: but not a word on 't now;
Here must no speeches pass, nor swords be drawn.   340

MATHIAS.

Suffer me, Barabas, but to follow him.

BARABAS.

No; so shall I, if any hurt be done,
Be made an accessory of your deeds.
Revenge it on him when you meet him next.

MATHIAS.

For this I'll have his heart.   345

BARABAS.

Do so; lo, here I give thee Abigail.

MATHIAS.

What greater gift can poor Mathias have?
Shall Lodowick rob me of so fair a love?
My life is not so dear as Abigail.

BARABAS.

My heart misgives me, that, to cross your love,   350
He's with your mother; therefore after him.

---

330. *resolv'd*] freed of uneasiness.
350. *My heart misgives me*] "I have a presentiment of evil" (Bennett).
350. *cross*] thwart.

MATHIAS.

    What, is he gone unto my mother?

BARABAS.

    Nay, if you will, stay till she comes herself.

MATHIAS.

    I cannot stay; for if my mother come,

    She'll die with grief.   *Exit.* 355

ABIGAIL.

    I cannot take my leave of him for tears.

    Father, why have you thus incens'd them both?

BARABAS.

    What's that to thee?

ABIGAIL.   I'll make 'em friends again.

BARABAS.

    You'll make 'em friends? Are there not Jews enow in Malta

    But thou must dote upon a Christian?   360

ABIGAIL.

    I will have Don Mathias; he is my love.

BARABAS.

    Yes, you shall have him. —Go, put her in.

ITHAMORE.

    Ay, I'll put her in.   [*Puts* Abigail *in.*]

BARABAS.

    Now tell me, Ithamore, how lik'st thou this?

ITHAMORE.

    Faith, master, I think by this you purchase both their lives; 365

    is it not so?

BARABAS.

    True; and it shall be cunningly perform'd.

ITHAMORE.

    O, master, that I might have a hand in this!

BARABAS.

    Ay, so thou shalt; 'tis thou must do the deed.

    Take this and bear it to Mathias straight,   370

    And tell him that it comes from Lodowick.

ITHAMORE.

    'Tis poison'd, is it not?

---

359. *enow*] enough.   365. *purchase*] get.
370. *straight*] immediately.

BARABAS.

No, no; and yet it might be done that way.
It is a challenge, feign'd from Lodowick.

ITHAMORE.

Fear not; I'll so set his heart afire that he shall verily think   375
it comes from him.

BARABAS.

I cannot choose but like thy readiness:
Yet be not rash, but do it cunningly.

ITHAMORE.

As I behave myself in this, employ me hereafter.

BARABAS.

Away then.   *Exit* [Ithamore]. 380
So, now will I go in to Lodowick,
And like a cunning spirit feign some lie,
Till I have set 'em both at enmity.   *Exit.*

[III.i]   *Enter* [Bellamira,] *a Courtesan.*

BELLAMIRA.

Since this town was besieg'd, my gain grows cold.
The time has been, that but for one bare night
A hundred ducats have been freely given;
But now against my will I must be chaste.
And yet I know my beauty doth not fail.   5
From Venice, merchants, and from Padua,
Were wont to come rare-witted gentlemen,
Scholars I mean, learned and liberal;
And now, save Pilia-Borza, comes there none,

[III.i]
1. S.P. BELLAMIRA] *Reed* (*subs.*);
not in Q.

---

377. *readiness*] prompt compliance, willingness.
[III.i]
0.1. *Courtesan*] prostitute.   1. *gain grows cold*] profit diminishes sharply.
3. *ducats*] coins "formerly in use in most European countries," varying
in value (*OED*).
6. *Venice*] once the greatest trading center in the Mediterranean.
6. *Padua*] the University of Padua was founded in 1228.
7. *rare-witted*] unusually intelligent.   8. *liberal*] generous.
9. *Pilia-Borza*] "A descriptive name analogous to the Italian *Taglia-borse*, a pickpocket" (Bennett).

And he is very seldom from my house.   10
And here he comes.

Enter Pilia-Borza.

PILIA-BORZA.

Hold thee, wench; there's something for thee to spend.

BELLAMIRA.

'Tis silver; I disdain it.

PILIA-BORZA.

Ay, but the Jew has gold,
And I will have it, or it shall go hard.   15

BELLAMIRA.

Tell me, how cam'st thou by this?

PILIA-BORZA.

Faith, walking the back lanes through the gardens I
chanc'd to cast mine eye up to the Jew's countinghouse,
where I saw some bags of money, and in the night I
clamber'd up with my hooks, and as I was taking my   20
choice, I heard a rumbling in the house; so I took only this,
and run my way. But here's the Jew's man.

Enter Ithamore.

BELLAMIRA.

Hide the bag.

PILIA-BORZA.

Look not towards him; let's away. Zounds, what a looking
thou keep'st; thou 'lt betray 's anon.   25

[*Exeunt* Bellamira *and* Pilia-Borza.]

ITHAMORE.

O, the sweetest face that ever I beheld! I know she is a
courtesan by her attire; now would I give a hundred of the
Jew's crowns that I had such a concubine. Well,
I have deliver'd the challenge in such sort,
As meet they will, and fighting die; brave sport.   *Exit.* 30

24. Zounds] *this edn.;* Zoon's *Q*.

---

10. *from*] away from.
12. *Hold thee*] hold out your hand (Kirschbaum).
20. *hooks*] apparently standard equipment for thieves.
24. *Zounds*] an oath, contracted from "by God's wounds."
24. *looking*] gaze.
27. *her attire*] Elizabethan courtesans customarily wore flowing, loose-bodied gowns.

[III.ii]   *Enter* Mathias.

MATHIAS.

>   This is the place; now Abigail shall see
>   Whether Mathias holds her dear or no.

Enter Lodowick, *reading.*

>   What, dares the villain write in such base terms?

LODOWICK.

>   I did it; and revenge it if thou dar'st!

[*They*] *fight. Enter* Barabas *above.*

BARABAS.

>   O, bravely fought! and yet they thrust not home.   5
>   Now, Lodowick! now, Mathias! So!   [*Both fall dead.*]
>   So now they have show'd themselves to be tall fellows.

[CRIES] WITHIN.

>   Part 'em! part 'em!

BARABAS.

>   Ay, part 'em now they are dead. Farewell, farewell.   *Exit.*

Enter Ferneze, Katherine [, *and Attendants*].

FERNEZE.

>   What sight is this? my Lodowick slain!   10
>   These arms of mine shall be thy sepulcher.

KATHERINE.

>   Who is this? my son Mathias slain!

FERNEZE.

>   O, Lodowick, hadst thou perish'd by the Turk,
>   Wretched Ferneze might have veng'd thy death.

KATHERINE.

>   Thy son slew mine, and I'll revenge his death.   15

FERNEZE.

>   Look, Katherine, look; thy son gave mine these wounds.

3.] *Dyce 1; Q repeats the speech*
prefix Math.

---

    7. *tall*] valiant (ironically), and with a play on the sense of their dead
bodies being stretched out at full length.
    10. *What sight*] what a sight.

KATHERINE.

O, leave to grieve me; I am griev'd enough.

FERNEZE.

O, that my sighs could turn to lively breath,
And these my tears to blood, that he might live.

KATHERINE.

Who made them enemies?   20

FERNEZE.

I know not; and that grieves me most of all.

KATHERINE.

My son lov'd thine.

FERNEZE.   And so did Lodowick him.

KATHERINE.

Lend me that weapon that did kill my son,
And it shall murder me.

FERNEZE.

Nay, madam, stay; that weapon was my son's,   25
And on that rather should Ferneze die.

KATHERINE.

Hold; let's inquire the causers of their deaths,
That we may venge their blood upon their heads.

FERNEZE.

Then take them up, and let them be interr'd
Within one sacred monument of stone,   30
Upon which altar I will offer up
My daily sacrifice of sighs and tears,
And with my prayers pierce impartial heavens,
Till they reveal the causers of our smarts,
Which forc'd their hands divide united hearts.   35
Come, Katherine, our losses equal are;
Then of true grief let us take equal share.

Exeunt [*with the bodies*].

34. reveal] *Dyce 1; not in Q.*   36. Katherine] *Reed; Katherina Q.*

---

17. *leave*] cease.   18. *lively*] living, hence, life-giving.
33. *impartial*] probably misused for *partial; OED* records two other
instances.
34. *smarts*] sorrows.
35. *Which*] has *causers* for antecedent.

[III.iii]   *Enter* Ithamore.

ITHAMORE.

Why, was there ever seen such villainy,
So neatly plotted, and so well perform'd?
Both held in hand, and flatly both beguil'd!

Enter Abigail.

ABIGAIL.

Why, how now, Ithamore, why laugh'st thou so?

ITHAMORE.

O, mistress, ha, ha, ha!   5

ABIGAIL.

Why, what ail'st thou?

ITHAMORE.

O, my master!

ABIGAIL.

Ha!

ITHAMORE.

O, mistress! I have the bravest, gravest, secret, subtle,
bottle-nos'd knave to my master that ever gentleman had.   10

ABIGAIL.

Say, knave, why rail'st upon my father thus?

ITHAMORE.

O, my master has the bravest policy.

ABIGAIL.

Wherein?

ITHAMORE.

Why, know you not?

ABIGAIL.

Why, no.   15

ITHAMORE.

Know you not of Mathias' and Don Lodowick's disaster?

16. Mathias'] *Reed; Mathia Q.*   16. Lodowick's] *Reed; Lodowick Q.*

---

3. *held in hand*] kept in expectation.   3. *flatly*] completely.
3. *beguil'd*] cheated.   9. *bravest*] most excellent.
9. *secret*] uncommunicative.   9. *subtle*] crafty.
10. *bottle-nos'd*] large-nosed; a common epithet (and attribute of the
devil in the morality plays).
10. *to*] for.   11. *rail'st upon*] utter abusive language about.

ABIGAIL.

No, what was it?

ITHAMORE.

Why, the devil invented a challenge, my master writ it, and
I carried it, first to Lodowick, and *imprimis* to Mathias.
And then they met, and as the story says,   20
In doleful wise they ended both their days.

ABIGAIL.

And was my father furtherer of their deaths?

ITHAMORE.

Am I Ithamore?

ABIGAIL.

Yes.

ITHAMORE.

So sure did your father write, and I carry the challenge.   25

ABIGAIL.

Well, Ithamore, let me request thee this:
Go to the new-made nunnery, and inquire
For any of the friars of St. Jacques,
And say I pray them come and speak with me.

ITHAMORE.

I pray, mistress, will you answer me to one question?   30

ABIGAIL.

Well, sirrah, what is 't?

ITHAMORE.

A very feeling one: have not the nuns fine sport with the
friars now and then?

ABIGAIL.

Go to, sirrah sauce; is this your question? Get ye gone.

ITHAMORE.

I will forsooth, mistress.   *Exit.*   35

19. Mathias] *Reed; Mathia Q.*   28. Jacques] *Scott* (Jaques); Iaynes
20. and] *Shone; not in Q.*   Q.

19. *imprimis*] first (Ithamore does not understand the meaning of the
word).

28. *friars of St. Jacques*] "The Dominicans or Black Friars were commonly
referred to as Jacobins, from their church of S. Jaques in Paris" (Bennett).

32. *feeling*] heart-felt.

34. *sirrah sauce*] the first term implies reprimand; the second is a word
for an impudent person.

ABIGAIL.

Hard-hearted father, unkind Barabas,
Was this the pursuit of thy policy?
To make me show them favor severally,
That by my favor they should both be slain?
Admit thou lov'dst not Lodowick for his sire,　　　40
Yet Don Mathias ne'er offended thee.
But thou wert set upon extreme revenge,
Because the prior dispossess'd thee once,
And couldst not venge it, but upon his son,
Nor on his son, but by Mathias' means,　　　45
Nor on Mathias, but by murdering me.
But I perceive there is no love on earth,
Pity in Jews, nor piety in Turks.
But here comes cursed Ithamore with the friar.

Enter Ithamore [*and*] Friar [Jacomo].

FRIAR JACOMO.

Virgo, salve.　　　50

ITHAMORE.

When! duck you?

ABIGAIL.

Welcome, grave friar; Ithamore, be gone.　　　*Exit* [Ithamore].
Know, holy sir, I am bold to solicit thee.

FRIAR JACOMO.

Wherein?

ABIGAIL.

To get me be admitted for a nun.　　　55

FRIAR JACOMO.

Why, Abigail, it is not yet long since
That I did labor thy admission,

40. sire] *Dyce 1;* sinne *Q.*

---

37. *pursuit*] aim.　　　38. *severally*] separately.
42. *extreme*] exceedingly harsh.
43. *prior*] "The title of a chief magistrate in some of the former Italian republics" (*OED*).
50. *Virgo, salve*] God save you, young woman (a greeting).
51. *When*] an exclamation of impatience.
51. *duck you?*] do you bow? (in obeisance).
57. *labor thy admission*] work hard for your acceptance (into the nunnery).

And then thou didst not like that holy life.

ABIGAIL.

    Then were my thoughts so frail and unconfirm'd,
    And I was chain'd to follies of the world;   60
    But now experience, purchased with grief,
    Has made me see the difference of things.
    My sinful soul, alas, hath pac'd too long
    The fatal labyrinth of misbelief,
    Far from the Son that gives eternal life.   65

FRIAR JACOMO.

    Who taught thee this?

ABIGAIL.   The Abbess of the house,
    Whose zealous admonition I embrace.
    O, therefore, Jacomo, let me be one,
    Although unworthy, of that sisterhood.

FRIAR JACOMO.

    Abigail, I will; but see thou change no more,   70
    For that will be most heavy to thy soul.

ABIGAIL.

    That was my father's fault.

FRIAR JACOMO.   Thy father's, how?

ABIGAIL.

    Nay, you shall pardon me. [aside] O, Barabas,
    Though thou deservest hardly at my hands,
    Yet never shall these lips bewray thy life.   75

FRIAR JACOMO.

    Come, shall we go?

ABIGAIL.   My duty waits on you.   *Exeunt.*

[III.iv]   *Enter* Barabas *reading a letter.*

BARABAS.

    What, Abigail become a nun again?
    False and unkind! What, hast thou lost thy father?

65. Son] *Reed;* Sonne *Q.*

---

   59. *unconfirm'd*] not yet made sure; ignorant.
   65. *Son*] with the common pun on *sun.*
   67. *admonition*] counsel.   67. *embrace*] accept joyfully.
   71. *heavy*] grievous.   74. *hardly*] harshly, severely.
   75. *bewray*] expose by divulging the secrets of.
[III.iv]
   2. *unkind*] unnatural; lacking in filial affection.

And all unknown, and unconstrain'd of me,
Art thou again got to the nunnery?
Now here she writes, and wills me to repent.   5
Repentance? *Spurca!* What pretendeth this?
I fear she knows ('tis so) of my device
In Don Mathias' and Lodovico's deaths:
If so, 'tis time that it be seen into,
For she that varies from me in belief   10
Gives great presumption that she loves me not;
Or loving, doth dislike of something done.
But who comes here?

[*Enter* Ithamore.]

O, Ithamore, come near;
Come near, my love; come near, thy master's life,
My trusty servant, nay, my second self,   15
For I have now no hope but even in thee,
And on that hope my happiness is built.
When saw'st thou Abigail?

ITHAMORE.   Today.

BARABAS.   With whom?

ITHAMORE.
A friar.

BARABAS.
A friar? false villain, he hath done the deed.   20

ITHAMORE.
How, sir?

BARABAS.   Why, made mine Abigail a nun.

ITHAMORE.
That's no lie, for she sent me for him.

BARABAS.
O, unhappy day!
False, credulous, inconstant Abigail!
But let 'em go; and, Ithamore, from hence   25
Ne'er shall she grieve me more with her disgrace;
Ne'er shall she live to inherit aught of mine,

15. self] *Penley;* life *Q*.

---

5. *wills*] desires.   6. *Spurca!*] filth!   6. *pretendeth*] means.
7. *device*] stratagem.   9. *seen into*] attended to.
11. *presumption*] reason for believing.   21. *How*] what.

Be bless'd of me, nor come within my gates,
But perish underneath my bitter curse,
Like Cain by Adam, for his brother's death.   30

ITHAMORE.

O, master!

BARABAS.

Ithamore, entreat not for her; I am mov'd,
And she is hateful to my soul and me:
And 'less thou yield to this that I entreat,
I cannot think but that thou hat'st my life.   35

ITHAMORE.

Who, I, master? Why I'll run to some rock
And throw myself headlong into the sea;
Why I'll do anything for your sweet sake.

BARABAS.

O, trusty Ithamore! no servant, but my friend;
I here adopt thee for mine only heir.   40
All that I have is thine when I am dead,
And whilst I live, use half; spend as myself.
Here, take my keys. I'll give 'em thee anon.
Go buy thee garments. But thou shalt not want.
Only know this, that thus thou art to do.   45
But first go fetch me in the pot of rice
That for our supper stands upon the fire.

ITHAMORE [aside].

I hold my head my master's hungry.—
I go, sir.   Exit.

BARABAS.

Thus every villain ambles after wealth,   50
Although he ne'er be richer than in hope.
But hush 't.

---

34. 'less] conj. Collier; least Q.   42. half] Reed; helfe Q.

---

28. within my gates] another biblical reminiscence; see, for example,
Deuteronomy 17 : 2.
30.] inaccurate; see Genesis 4 : 9–16.
32. mov'd] provoked to anger.
43. anon] soon.
45.] i.e., in some purposely vague future.
48. hold] bet, wager.
50. ambles] moves easily (like an ambling horse).

Enter Ithamore *with the pot.*

ITHAMORE.   Here 'tis, master.

BARABAS.   Well said, Ithamore.

What, hast thou brought the ladle with thee too?

ITHAMORE.

Yes, sir; the proverb says, he that eats with the devil had
need of a long spoon. I have brought you a ladle.   55

BARABAS.

Very well, Ithamore; then now be secret,
And for thy sake, whom I so dearly love,
Now shalt thou see the death of Abigail,
That thou mayst freely live to be my heir.

ITHAMORE.

Why, master, will you poison her with a mess of rice   60
porridge? That will preserve life, make her round and
plump, and batten more than you are aware.

BARABAS.

Ay, but, Ithamore, seest thou this?
It is a precious powder that I bought
Of an Italian in Ancona once,   65
Whose operation is to bind, infect,
And poison deeply, yet not appear
In forty hours after it is ta'en.

ITHAMORE.

How, master?

BARABAS.

Thus, Ithamore: 70
This even they use in Malta here ('tis call'd
Saint Jacques' Even) and then, I say, they use
To send their alms unto the nunneries;
Among the rest, bear this, and set it there.
There's a dark entry where they take it in,   75
Where they must neither see the messenger,
Nor make inquiry who hath sent it them.

---

52. *Well said*] well done.
60. *mess*] serving.   62. *batten*] thrive.
65. *Ancona*] port city in Italy which provided asylum for Portuguese Jews.
66. *bind*] constipate.
72. *they use*] the inhabitants are accustomed.

ITHAMORE.

How so?

BARABAS.

Belike there is some ceremony in 't.

There, Ithamore, must thou go place this pot;.   80

Stay, let me spice it first.

ITHAMORE.

Pray do, and let me help you, master. Pray let me taste first.

BARABAS.

Prithee, do. What say'st thou now?

ITHAMORE.

Troth, master, I'm loath such a pot of pottage should

be spoil'd.   85

BARABAS.

Peace, Ithamore; 'tis better so than spar'd.

Assure thyself thou shalt have broth by the eye.

My purse, my coffer, and myself is thine.

ITHAMORE.

Well, master, I go.

BARABAS.

Stay, first let me stir it, Ithamore.   90

As fatal be it to her as the draught

Of which great Alexander drunk, and died;

And with her let it work like Borgia's wine,

Whereof his sire, the Pope, was poison'd.

In few, the blood of Hydra, Lerna's bane,   95

---

80. pot] *Reed;* plot *Q.*

84. *pottage*] thick soup.

86. *spar'd*] saved, reserved.

87. *by the eye*] in unlimited quantity.

92. *Alexander*] Cooper records that he was poisoned for his "cruelty and pride," reputedly by Aristotle, his former teacher, and Antipater, his lieutenant.

93. *Borgia*] Cesare Borgia, reputed to have poisoned his father, Pope Alexander VI (died 1503).

95. *In few*] in short.

95. *Hydra*] many-headed monster, killed by Hercules; its blood was poisonous.

95. *Lerna's bane*] that which poisoned Lerna, the marsh near Argos where the Hydra lived.

The juice of hebon, and Cocytus' breath,
And all the poisons of the Stygian pool
Break from the fiery kingdom, and in this
Vomit your venom, and envenom her
That like a fiend hath left her father thus.   100

ITHAMORE.

What a blessing has he giv'n 't! Was ever pot of rice porridge
so sauc'd? What shall I do with it?

BARABAS.

O, my sweet Ithamore, go set it down
And come again so soon as thou hast done,
For I have other business for thee.   105

ITHAMORE.

Here's a drench to poison a whole stable of Flanders mares.
I'll carry 't to the nuns with a powder.

BARABAS.

And the horse pestilence to boot; away!

ITHAMORE.

I am gone.
Pay me my wages, for my work is done.   *Exit.* 110

BARABAS.

I'll pay thee with a vengeance, Ithamore.   *Exit.*

[III.v]

Enter Ferneze, [Martin del] Bosco, *Knights,* [*and*] Callapine.

FERNEZE.

Welcome, great bashaw; how fares Calymath?
What wind drives you thus into Malta road?

CALLAPINE.

The wind that bloweth all the world besides:

0.1. Callapine] *this edn.; Bashaw Q.*   1. bashaw] *Reed; Bashaws Q.*

---

96. *hebon*] a poisonous plant, possibly the yew.
96. *Cocytus' breath*] vapor given off by Cocytus, one of the rivers of Hades.
97. *Stygian pool*] a well of Arcadia, whose water was an extremely cold and extremely strong poison (Cooper).
98. *the fiery kingdom*] i.e., hell.   102. *sauc'd*] seasoned.
106. *drench*] dose of medicine (usually with reference to animals).
106. *Flanders*] Belgian.
107. *with a powder*] quickly (with an obvious pun).
108. *to boot*] besides.

Desire of gold.

FERNEZE.   Desire of gold, great sir?

That's to be gotten in the Western Inde: 5

In Malta are no golden minerals.

CALLAPINE.

To you of Malta thus saith Calymath:

The time you took for respite is at hand

For the performance of your promise past;

And for the tribute money I am sent.   10

FERNEZE.

Bashaw, in brief, shalt have no tribute here,

Nor shall the heathens live upon our spoil.

First will we raze the city walls ourselves,

Lay waste the island, hew the temples down,

And shipping of our goods to Sicily,   15

Open an entrance for the wasteful sea,

Whose billows, beating the resistless banks,

Shall overflow it with their refluence.

CALLAPINE.

Well, governor, since thou hast broke the league

By flat denial of the promis'd tribute,   20

Talk not of razing down your city walls;

You shall not need trouble yourselves so far,

For Selim Calymath shall come himself,

And with brass bullets batter down your towers,

And turn proud Malta to a wilderness   25

For these intolerable wrongs of yours.

And so, farewell.

FERNEZE.

Farewell.   [*Exit* Callapine.]

And now, you men of Malta, look about,

And let's provide to welcome Calymath.   30

Close your portcullis, charge your basilisks,

And as you profitably take up arms,

So now courageously encounter them;

For by this answer, broken is the league,

---

16. *wasteful*] causing destruction.   17. *resistless*] irresistible.

18. *refluence*] flowing back, ebbing.   31. *basilisks*] large brass cannon.

32. *profitably*] for your own advantage.

And naught is to be look'd for now but wars,   35
And naught to us more welcome is than wars.   *Exeunt.*

[III.vi]   *Enter two* Friars [, Jacomo and Barnardine].

FRIAR JACOMO.
     O, brother, brother, all the nuns are sick,
     And physic will not help them; they must die.
FRIAR BARNARDINE.
     The Abbess sent for me to be confess'd:
     O, what a sad confession will there be!
FRIAR JACOMO.
     And so did fair Maria send for me.   5
     I'll to her lodging; hereabouts she lies.   *Exit.*

                    Enter Abigail.

FRIAR BARNARDINE.
     What, all dead save only Abigail?
ABIGAIL.
     And I shall die too, for I feel death coming.
     Where is the friar that convers'd with me?
FRIAR BARNARDINE.
     O, he is gone to see the other nuns.   10
ABIGAIL.
     I sent for him, but seeing you are come,
     Be you my ghostly father; and first know
     That in this house I liv'd religiously,
     Chaste, and devout, much sorrowing for my sins,
     But ere I came—   15
FRIAR BARNARDINE.
     What then?
ABIGAIL.
     I did offend high heaven so grievously
     As I am almost desperate for my sins;
     And one offense torments me more than all.
     You knew Mathias and Don Lodowick?   20

0.1.] *Reed (subs.); Enter two Fryars
and Abigall. Q.*

2. *physic*] medicine.   12. *ghostly father*] father confessor.

FRIAR BARNARDINE.

Yes, what of them?

ABIGAIL.

My father did contract me to 'em both:
First to Don Lodowick. Him I never lov'd.
Mathias was the man that I held dear,
And for his sake did I become a nun.   25

FRIAR BARNARDINE.

So; say how was their end?

ABIGAIL.

Both, jealous of my love, envied each other,
And by my father's practice, which is there   [*Gives a paper.*]
Set down at large, the gallants were both slain.

FRIAR BARNARDINE.

O, monstrous villainy!   30

ABIGAIL.

To work my peace, this I confess to thee;
Reveal it not, for then my father dies.

FRIAR BARNARDINE.

Know that confession must not be reveal'd;
The canon law forbids it, and the priest
That makes it known, being degraded first,   35
Shall be condemn'd, and then sent to the fire.

ABIGAIL.

So I have heard; pray, therefore, keep it close.
Death seizeth on my heart. Ah, gentle friar,
Convert my father, that he may be sav'd,
And witness that I die a Christian.   [*Dies.*] 40

FRIAR BARNARDINE.

Ay, and a virgin, too; that grieves me most.
But I must to the Jew and exclaim on him,
And make him stand in fear of me.

Enter 1 Friar [Jacomo].

FRIAR JACOMO.   O, brother,

---

22. *contract*] engage, betroth.   27. *envied*] felt a grudge against.
28. *practice*] trick.   29. *at large*] at length, in full.
29. *gallants*] brave gentlemen.   31. *work*] bring about.
35. *degraded*] stripped of ecclesiastical orders; defrocked.
37. *close*] secret.   42. *exclaim on him*] accuse him vociferously.

All the nuns are dead; let's bury them.

FRIAR BARNARDINE.

First help to bury this, then go with me   45
And help me to exclaim against the Jew.

FRIAR JACOMO.

Why? what has he done?

FRIAR BARNARDINE.

A thing that makes me tremble to unfold.

FRIAR JACOMO.

What, has he crucified a child?

FRIAR BARNARDINE.

No, but a worse thing. 'Twas told me in shrift;   50
Thou know'st 'tis death and if it be reveal'd.
Come, let's away.   *Exeunt [with the body].*

[IV.i]   *Enter* Barabas [*and*] Ithamore. *Bells within.*

BARABAS.

There is no music to a Christian's knell.
How sweet the bells ring now the nuns are dead
That sound at other times like tinkers' pans!
I was afraid the poison had not wrought;
Or, though it wrought, it would have done no good,   5
For every year they swell, and yet they live.
Now all are dead; not one remains alive.

ITHAMORE.

That's brave, master, but think you it will not be known?

BARABAS.

How can it if we two be secret?

ITHAMORE.

For my part fear you not.   10

BARABAS.

I'd cut thy throat if I did.

ITHAMORE.   And reason, too.

---

46. *exclaim against*] make an outcry against.
49. *crucified a child*] Jews were reputed to do so.
50. *shrift*] confession.   51. *and if*] if.
[IV.i]
1. *to*] compared to.   4. *wrought*] produced its effect.
6.] one of a number of allusions to the promiscuity of the nuns.
8. *brave*] fine.

But here's a royal monast'ry hard by;
Good master, let me poison all the monks.

BARABAS.

Thou shalt not need, for now the nuns are dead,
They'll die with grief.   15

ITHAMORE.

Do you not sorrow for your daughter's death?

BARABAS.

No, but I grieve because she liv'd so long.
An Hebrew born, and would become a Christian!
Cazzo! diabolo!

Enter the two Friars [, Jacomo *and* Barnardine].

ITHAMORE.

Look, look, master; here come two religious caterpillars.   20

BARABAS.

I smelt 'em ere they came.

ITHAMORE.

God-a-mercy, nose; come, let's be gone.

FRIAR BARNARDINE.

Stay, wicked Jew; repent, I say, and stay.

FRIAR JACOMO.

Thou hast offended, therefore must be damn'd.

BARABAS.

I fear they know we sent the poison'd broth.   25

ITHAMORE.

And so do I, master; therefore speak 'em fair.

FRIAR BARNARDINE.

Barabas, thou hast—

FRIAR JACOMO.

Ay, that thou hast—

BARABAS.

True, I have money; what though I have?

FRIAR BARNARDINE.

Thou art a—   30

19. *Cazzo*] Dyce 1; Catho Q.   19. *diabolo*] Collier; diabola Q.

---

12. *royal*] first-rate.   19. *Cazzo!*] an Italian obscenity.
19. *diabolo!*] the devil!
20. *caterpillars*] contemptuous term meaning persons who prey upon
society.

FRIAR JACOMO.

Ay, that thou art, a—

BARABAS.

What needs all this? I know I am a Jew.

FRIAR BARNARDINE.

Thy daughter—

FRIAR JACOMO.

Ay, thy daughter—

BARABAS.

O, speak not of her; then I die with grief.   35

FRIAR BARNARDINE.

Remember that—

FRIAR JACOMO.

Ay, remember that—

BARABAS.

I must needs say that I have been a great usurer.

FRIAR BARNARDINE.

Thou hast committed—

BARABAS.

Fornication? but that was in another country: and besides,   40
the wench is dead.

FRIAR BARNARDINE.

Ay, but Barabas, remember Mathias and Don Lodowick.

BARABAS.

Why, what of them?

FRIAR BARNARDINE.

I will not say that by a forged challenge they met.

BARABAS (*aside*).

She has confess'd, and we are both undone;   45
My bosom inmates! but I must dissemble.
—O, holy friars, the burden of my sins
Lie heavy on my soul. Then, pray you, tell me,
Is 't not too late now to turn Christian?
I have been zealous in the Jewish faith,   50
Hard-hearted to the poor, a covetous wretch,
That would for lucre's sake have sold my soul.

45. *aside*] *Neilson;   at   right-hand*
margin after l. 46, Q.

46. *My bosom inmates*] "*I.e.*, the friars are now in my secrets" (Spencer).

A hundred for a hundred I have ta'en,
And now for store of wealth may I compare
With all the Jews in Malta. But what is wealth?   55
I am a Jew, and therefore am I lost.
Would penance serve for this my sin,
I could afford to whip myself to death.

ITHAMORE.

And so could I; but penance will not serve.

BARABAS.

To fast, to pray, and wear a shirt of hair,   60
And on my knees creep to Jerusalem;
Cellars of wine, and sollars full of wheat,
Warehouses stuff'd with spices and with drugs,
Whole chests of gold, in bullion, and in coin,
Besides I know not how much weight in pearl,   65
Orient and round, have I within my house;
At Alexandria, merchandise unsold;
But yesterday two ships went from this town;
Their voyage will be worth ten thousand crowns.
In Florence, Venice, Antwerp, London, Seville,   70
Frankfort, Lubeck, Moscow, and where not,
Have I debts owing, and, in most of these,
Great sums of money lying in the banco.
All this I'll give to some religious house,
So I may be baptiz'd and live therein.   75

FRIAR JACOMO.

O, good Barabas, come to our house!

FRIAR BARNARDINE.

O no, good Barabas, come to our house!
And, Barabas, you know—

BARABAS [to Barnardine].

I know that I have highly sinn'd.
You shall convert me; you shall have all my wealth.   80

64. bullion] *Reed; Bulloine Q.*

53.] I have charged 100 per cent interest.
62. *sollars*] lofts.
63. *drugs*] "ingredients used in chemistry, pharmacy, dyeing, and the arts generally" (*OED*).
73. *banco*] commercial office; bank.   75. *So*] provided that.

FRIAR JACOMO.

O, Barabas, their laws are strict.

BARABAS [*to* Jacomo].

I know they are, and I will be with you.

FRIAR BARNARDINE.

They wear no shirts, and they go barefoot, too.

BARABAS [*to* Barnardine].

Then 'tis not for me; and I am resolv'd

You shall confess me, and have all my goods.   85

FRIAR JACOMO.

Good Barabas, come to me.

BARABAS [*aside to* Jacomo].

You see I answer him, and yet he stays;

Rid him away, and go you home with me.

FRIAR JACOMO [*aside to* Barabas].

I'll be with you tonight.

BARABAS [*aside to* Jacomo].

Come to my house at one o'clock this night.   90

FRIAR JACOMO.

You hear your answer, and you may be gone.

FRIAR BARNARDINE.

Why, go, get you away.

FRIAR JACOMO.

I will not go for thee.

FRIAR BARNARDINE.

Not! then I'll make thee go.

FRIAR JACOMO.

How, dost call me rogue?   [*They*] *fight.* 95

ITHAMORE.

Part 'em, master, part 'em!

BARABAS.

This is mere frailty, brethren; be content.

Friar Barnardine, go you with Ithamore.

83. S.P. FRIAR BARNARDINE] *Reed*   89. S.P. FRIAR JACOMO] *Dyce 1;*
(*subs.*); *1. Q.*   *2. Q.*

---

88. *Rid him away*] get rid of him (violently).
93. *for*] on account of.
95. *rogue*] Jacomo misunderstands Barnardine's *go.*

[*aside to* Barnardine] You know my mind; let me alone
    with him.

FRIAR JACOMO.

Why does he go to thy house? Let him be gone.   100

BARABAS [*aside to* Jacomo].

I'll give him something, and so stop his mouth.
                Exit [Ithamore *with* Friar Barnardine].
I never heard of any man but he
Malign'd the order of the Jacobins;
But do you think that I believe his words?
Why, brother, you converted Abigail,   105
And I am bound in charity to requite it;
And so I will. O, Jacomo, fail not, but come.

FRIAR JACOMO.

But, Barabas, who shall be your godfathers? For presently
you shall be shriv'd.

BARABAS.

Marry, the Turk shall be one of my godfathers: but not   110
a word to any of your covent.

FRIAR JACOMO.

I warrant thee, Barabas.   *Exit.*

BARABAS.

So now the fear is past, and I am safe:
For he that shriv'd her is within my house.
What if I murder'd him ere Jacomo comes?   115
Now I have such a plot for both their lives
As never Jew nor Christian knew the like.
One turn'd my daughter, therefore he shall die;
The other knows enough to have my life,
Therefore 'tis not requisite he should live.   120
But are not both these wise men to suppose
That I will leave my house, my goods, and all,
To fast and be well whipp'd? I'll none of that.

99–100.] *Dyce 1; both lines assigned*
to Ith. Q.

99. *let me alone with him*] "Leave me to deal with him" (Spencer).
103. *Jacobins*] Dominicans.   110. *the Turk*] Ithamore.
111. *covent*] convent, religious house.
112. *warrant*] assure.   118. *turn'd*] converted.
120.] therefore 'tis requisite he should not live.

Now, Friar Barnardine, I come to you.
I'll feast you, lodge you, give you fair words,   125
And after that, I and my trusty Turk—
No more but so: it must and shall be done.
Ithamore, tell me, is the friar asleep?

Enter Ithamore.

ITHAMORE.

Yes; and I know not what the reason is:
Do what I can, he will not strip himself,   130
Nor go to bed, but sleeps in his own clothes;
I fear me he mistrusts what we intend.

BARABAS.

No, 'tis an order which the friars use.
Yet if he knew our meanings, could he 'scape?

ITHAMORE.

No, none can hear him, cry he ne'er so loud.   135

BARABAS.

Why, true; therefore did I place him there:
The other chambers open towards the street.

ITHAMORE.

You loiter, master; wherefore stay we thus?
O, how I long to see him shake his heels.

BARABAS.

Come on, sirrah.   140
Off with your girdle; make a handsome noose.
Friar, awake!

          [*Draws curtains of the inner stage, revealing* Barnardine *asleep.*]

FRIAR BARNARDINE.

What, do you mean to strangle me?

ITHAMORE.

Yes, 'cause you use to confess.

BARABAS.

Blame not us but the proverb, "Confess and be hang'd."   145
Pull hard!

---

127. *No more but so*] "that's that."   132. *mistrusts*] suspects.
133. *order*] customary practice.
139. *shake his heels*] i.e., be hanged.   141. *girdle*] belt.
144. *use to confess*] are accustomed to hear confession.

FRIAR BARNARDINE.

 What, will you have my life?

BARABAS.

 Pull hard, I say; you would have had my goods.

ITHAMORE.

 Ay, and our lives, too; therefore pull amain.

                                    [Friar Barnardine *dies.*]

 'Tis neatly done, sir; here's no print at all.   150

BARABAS.

 Then is it as it should be; take him up.

ITHAMORE.

 Nay, master, be rul'd by me a little. So, let him lean upon
 his staff; excellent, he stands as if he were begging of bacon.

BARABAS.

 Who would not think but that this friar liv'd?
 What time a' night is 't now, sweet Ithamore?   155

ITHAMORE.

 Towards one.

BARABAS.

 Then will not Jacomo be long from hence.

                                    [*Exit.* Ithamore *hides.*]

                    Enter [Friar] Jacomo.

FRIAR JACOMO.

 This is the hour wherein I shall proceed;
 O, happy hour, wherein I shall convert
 An infidel, and bring his gold into our treasury.   160
 But soft, is not this Barnardine? It is;
 And, understanding I should come this way,
 Stands here a' purpose, meaning me some wrong,
 And intercept my going to the Jew.
 Barnardine!   165
 Wilt thou not speak? Thou think'st I see thee not.
 Away, I'd wish thee, and let me go by.
 No, wilt thou not? Nay, then, I'll force my way;
 And see, a staff stands ready for the purpose:

---

147. have] *Shone;* saue *Q.*   157.2.] *Reed; after l. 156 Q.*

149. *amain*] with full force.
150. *no print*] no mark of the belt on his neck.
158. *proceed*] prosper.   161. *soft*] wait a moment.

As thou lik'st that, stop me another time!   170

Strike him, he falls. Enter Barabas.

BARABAS.

Why, how now, Jacomo, what hast thou done?

FRIAR JACOMO.

Why, stricken him that would have stroke at me.

BARABAS.

Who is it? Barnardine? Now out, alas, he is slain.

ITHAMORE.

Ay, master, he's slain; look how his brains drop out on's
nose.   175

FRIAR JACOMO.

Good sirs, I have done 't, but nobody knows it but you two.
I may escape.

BARABAS.

So might my man and I hang with you for company.

ITHAMORE.

No, let us bear him to the magistrates.

FRIAR JACOMO.

Good Barabas, let me go.   180

BARABAS.

No, pardon me; the law must have his course.
I must be forc'd to give in evidence
That being importun'd by this Barnardine
To be a Christian, I shut him out,
And there he sat. Now I, to keep my word,   185
And give my goods and substance to your house,
Was up thus early, with intent to go
Unto your friary, because you stay'd.

ITHAMORE.

Fie upon 'em! Master, will you turn Christian, when
holy friars turn devils and murder one another?   190

BARABAS.

No, for this example I'll remain a Jew.

---

173. *Now out*] an interjection expressing abhorrence.
174. *on's*] of his.   181. *his*] its.
186. *substance*] possessions, wealth.
188. *stay'd*] tarried, delayed.

Heaven bless me! what, a friar a murderer?
When shall you see a Jew commit the like?

ITHAMORE.

Why, a Turk could ha' done no more.

BARABAS.

Tomorrow is the sessions; you shall to it.   195
Come, Ithamore, let's help to take him hence.

FRIAR JACOMO.

Villains, I am a sacred person. Touch me not.

BARABAS.

The law shall touch you; we'll but lead you, we.
'Las, I could weep at your calamity.
Take in the staff too, for that must be shown: 200
Law wills that each particular be known. *Exeunt [with the body].*

[IV.ii]   *Enter* Bellamira *and* Pilia-Borza.

BELLAMIRA.

Pilia-Borza, didst thou meet with Ithamore?

PILIA-BORZA.

I did.

BELLAMIRA.

And didst thou deliver my letter?

PILIA-BORZA.

I did.

BELLAMIRA.

And what think'st thou, will he come?   5

PILIA-BORZA.

I think so, and yet I cannot tell, for at the reading of the
letter, he look'd like a man of another world.

BELLAMIRA.

Why so?

PILIA-BORZA.

That such a base slave as he should be saluted by such a
tall man as I am, from such a beautiful dame as you.   10

---

101. *sessions*] judicial sitting.   198. *touch*] charge.
201. *wills*] decrees.   201. *particular*] individual item.
[IV.ii]
    9. *saluted*] greeted.   10. *tall*] handsome.

BELLAMIRA.

And what said he?

PILIA-BORZA.

Not a wise word, only gave me a nod, as who should say,
"Is it even so?" and so I left him, being driven to a non-plus
at the critical aspect of my terrible countenance.

BELLAMIRA.

And where didst meet him?   15

PILIA-BORZA.

Upon mine own freehold, within forty foot of the gallows,
conning his neck-verse, I take it, looking of a friar's execution, whom I saluted with an old hempen proverb, *hodie*
tibi, cras mihi, and so I left him to the mercy of the hangman. But the exercise being done, see where he comes.   20

Enter Ithamore.

ITHAMORE.

I never knew a man take his death so patiently as this friar.
He was ready to leap off ere the halter was about his neck;
and when the hangman had put on his hempen tippet, he
made such haste to his prayers as if he had had another
cure to serve. Well, go whither he will, I'll be none of his   25
followers in haste. And now I think on 't, going to the
execution, a fellow met me with a muschatoes like a raven's
wing, and a dagger with a hilt like a warming pan, and he
gave me a letter from one Madam Bellamira, saluting me in
such sort as if he had meant to make clean my boots with his 30

18. *hodie*] Q. *corr.* (*Hodie*); *Hidie* Q
uncorr.

---

13. *non-plus*] state of perplexity.   14. *critical aspect*] censorious gaze.

16. *freehold*] estate held for life—Pilia-Borza's "own territory."

17. *conning his neck-verse*] studying the Latin text set before him in
claiming benefit of clergy (freedom from penalty imposed by a secular
court; the ability to read established one's right to the benefit).

17. *looking of*] watching.

18. *hempen*] humorously, in reference to the hangman's halter.

18–19. *hodie tibi, cras mihi*] your turn today, mine tomorrow.

20. *exercise*] act of public worship (humorously).

23. *hempen tippet*] jocularly, the hangman's noose; a *tippet* is a long scarf
worn around the neck by a clergyman as part of his vestments.

25. *cure to serve*] parish to minister to.   27. *muschatoes*] mustache.

29–31. *saluting...lips*] i.e., greeting me with a very low bow.

lips. The effect was that I should come to her house. I
wonder what the reason is? It may be she sees more in me
than I can find in myself; for she writes further, that she
loves me ever since she saw me, and who would not requite
such love? Here's her house, and here she comes, and now   35
would I were gone; I am not worthy to look upon her.

PILIA-BORZA.

This is the gentleman you writ to.

ITHAMORE [aside].

"Gentleman!" he flouts me; what gentry can be in a poor
Turk of ten pence? I'll be gone.

BELLAMIRA.

Is 't not a sweet-fac'd youth, Pilia?   40

ITHAMORE [aside].

Again, "sweet youth!"—Did not you, sir, bring the sweet
youth a letter?

PILIA-BORZA.

I did, sir, and from this gentlewoman, who, as myself and
the rest of the family, stand or fall at your service.

BELLAMIRA.

Though woman's modesty should hale me back, I can with-   45
hold no longer: welcome, sweet love.

ITHAMORE [aside].

Now am I clean, or rather foully, out of the way.

BELLAMIRA.

Whither so soon?

ITHAMORE [aside].

I'll go steal some money from my master to make me
handsome. —Pray, pardon me, I must go see a ship   50
discharg'd.

BELLAMIRA.

Canst thou be so unkind to leave me thus?

PILIA-BORZA.

And ye did but know how she loves you, sir!

---

31. *effect*] purport.   38. *flouts*] mocks.
39. *Turk of ten pence*] i.e., a worthless Turk.   45. *hale*] pull.
47. *clean*] completely (with a pun, to pair with *foully*).
47. *out of the way*] off the track.   51. *discharg'd*] unloaded.
53. *And*] if.

ITHAMORE.

 Nay, I care not how much she loves me. —Sweet Bellamira,
would I had my master's wealth for thy sake.   55

PILIA-BORZA.

 And you can have it, sir, and if you please.

ITHAMORE.

 If 'twere above ground I could, and would have it; but he
hides and buries it up as partridges do their eggs, under the
earth.

PILIA-BORZA.

 And is 't not possible to find it out?   60

ITHAMORE.

 By no means possible.

BELLAMIRA [*aside to* Pilia-Borza].

 What shall we do with this base villain then?

PILIA-BORZA [*aside to her*].

 Let me alone; do but you speak him fair.—
 But you know some secrets of the Jew,
 Which if they were reveal'd would do him harm. 65

ITHAMORE.

 Ay, and such as—go to, no more! I'll make him send me
half he has, and glad he 'scapes so, too. Pen and ink! I'll
write unto him. We'll have money straight.

PILIA-BORZA.

 Send for a hundred crowns at least.

ITHAMORE.

 Ten hundred thousand crowns. (*He writes.*) "Master Barabas." 70

PILIA-BORZA.

 Write not so submissively, but threat'ning him.

ITHAMORE.

 "Sirrah Barabas, send me a hundred crowns."

PILIA-BORZA.

 Put in two hundred at least.

54. Bellamira] *Reed; Allamira Q*. 70. *He writes*] *Dyce 1 (subs.); in
blank space above* Mr. Barabas *Q*.

56. *and if*] if. 63. *Let me alone*] leave it to me.
63. *speak him fair*] talk sweetly to him.
66. *go to*] come, come. 68. *straight*] immediately.

ITHAMORE.

"I charge thee send me three hundred by this bearer, and
this shall be your warrant; if you do not, no more but so."   75

PILIA-BORZA.

Tell him you will confess.

ITHAMORE.

"Otherwise I'll confess all." Vanish and return in a twinkle.

PILIA-BORZA.

Let me alone; I'll use him in his kind.   [*Exit.*]

ITHAMORE.

Hang him, Jew.

BELLAMIRA.

Now, gentle Ithamore, lie in my lap.   80
Where are my maids? Provide a running banquet.
Send to the merchant, bid him bring me silks;
Shall Ithamore my love go in such rags?

ITHAMORE.

And bid the jeweler come hither too.

BELLAMIRA.

I have no husband, sweet; I'll marry thee.   85

ITHAMORE.

Content; but we will leave this paltry land,
And sail from hence to Greece, to lovely Greece.
I'll be thy Jason, thou my golden fleece;
Where painted carpets o'er the meads are hurl'd,
And Bacchus' vineyards o'erspread the world;   90
Where woods and forests go in goodly green,
I'll be Adonis, thou shalt be Love's Queen.
The meads, the orchards, and the primrose lanes,
Instead of sedge and reed, bear sugar canes:

---

77. *return in a twinkle*] "A conjuring phrase" (Bennett).
78. *in his kind*] according to his (1) nature (2) race—i.e., as he deserves.
81. *running banquet*] quick snack.   86. *Content*] agreed.
88. *Jason*] in Greek mythology, leader of the Argonauts, who ultimately
recovered the magical golden fleece.
89. *painted carpets*] i.e.; many-colored expanses of flowers.
89. *meads*] meadows.
90. *Bacchus*] Roman name for Dionysus, god of wine.
92. *Adonis*] famous lover of Venus (Love's Queen).
94. *sedge*] a coarse, grassy plant.

Thou in those groves, by Dis above,   95
Shalt live with me and be my love.

BELLAMIRA.

Whither will I not go with gentle Ithamore?

Enter Pilia-Borza.

ITHAMORE.

How now? hast thou the gold?

PILIA-BORZA.

Yes.

ITHAMORE.

But came it freely? Did the cow give down her milk freely? 100

PILIA-BORZA.

At reading of the letter, he star'd and stamp'd and turn'd
aside. I took him by the beard, and look'd upon him thus;
told him he were best to send it; then he hugg'd and
embrac'd me.

ITHAMORE.

Rather for fear than love.   105

PILIA-BORZA.

Then, like a Jew, he laugh'd and jeer'd, and told me he
lov'd me for your sake, and said what a faithful servant you
had been.

ITHAMORE.

The more villain he to keep me thus. Here's goodly 'parel,
is there not?   110

PILIA-BORZA.

To conclude, he gave me ten crowns.

ITHAMORE.

But ten? I'll not leave him worth a gray groat. Give me a

102. beard] *Reed;* sterd *Q.*

---

95. *Dis*] Roman god of the underworld; Ithamore's oath humorously
reveals his ignorance.

100. *give down*] let flow; a term from dairying.

101 *star'd and stamp'd*] "denoting the indications of uncontrolled rage"
(*OED*).

102. *took him by the beard*] a great insult in Elizabethan times.

109. *'parel*] apparel.

111. *gave me ten crowns*] apparently as a tip or bribe (Bennett).

112. *gray groat*] "the type of something of little value" (*OED*).

ream of paper; we'll have a kingdom of gold for 't.

PILIA-BORZA.

Write for five hundred crowns.

ITHAMORE.

"Sirrah Jew, as you love your life, send me five hundred   115
crowns, and give the bearer one hundred." Tell him I
must have 't.

PILIA-BORZA.

I warrant your worship shall have 't.

ITHAMORE.

And if he ask why I demand so much, tell him I scorn to
write a line under a hundred crowns.   120

PILIA-BORZA.

You'd make a rich poet, sir. I am gone.   *Exit.*

ITHAMORE.

Take thou the money; spend it for my sake.

BELLAMIRA.

'Tis not thy money, but thyself I weigh:
Thus Bellamira esteems of gold: *[Throws it aside.]*
But thus of thee—   *Kiss him.*

ITHAMORE.   That kiss again; she runs   125
Division of my lips. What an eye
She casts on me! It twinkles like a star.

BELLAMIRA.

Come, my dear love, let's in and sleep together.

ITHAMORE.

O, that ten thousand nights were put in one,
That we might sleep seven years together afore we wake.   130

BELLAMIRA.

Come, amorous wag; first banquet, and then sleep.   *[Exeunt.]*

---

113. *ream*] with a pun on *realm*, similarly pronounced in Elizabethan
English.

123. *weigh*] ascribe value to.

125–126. *runs/ Division of my lips*] lavishes "kisses on him with passionate
iteration and variation" (Bennett); the metaphor is from music, to *run
division* meaning "to execute a rapid melodic passage" (*OED*).

127. *twinkles*] with a play on the meaning *winks* (of the eye).

131. *wag*] young fellow; here, a term of endearment.

[IV.iii]   *Enter* Barabas *reading a letter.*

BARABAS.

"Barabas, send me three hundred crowns."
Plain Barabas! O, that wicked courtesan!
He was not wont to call me Barabas.
"Or else I will confess." Ay, there it goes.
But if I get him, *coupe de gorge*. For that   5
He sent a shaggy, totter'd, staring slave,
That when he speaks, draws out his grisly beard,
And winds it twice or thrice about his ear;
Whose face has been a grindstone for men's swords;
His hands are hack'd, some fingers cut quite off;   10
Who when he speaks, grunts like a hog, and looks
Like one that is employ'd in catzerie
And crossbiting; such a rogue
As is the husband to a hundred whores—
And I by him must send three hundred crowns!   15
Well, my hope is he will not stay there still;
And when he comes—O, that he were but here!

                Enter Pilia-Borza.

PILIA-BORZA.

Jew, I must ha' more gold.

BARABAS.

Why, want'st thou any of thy tale?

PILIA-BORZA.

No; but three hundred will not serve his turn.   20

BARABAS.

Not serve his turn, sir?

---

5. *coupe de gorge*] cut the throat.
6. *totter'd*] tattered.   6. *staring*] wild.
7. *grisly*] horrible (or, possibly, *grizzly*, "grayish, grizzled").
12. *catzerie*] ? probably derived from the same Italian obscenity as *cazzo* (IV.i.19. above); ? whoremongering.
13. *crossbiting*] swindling.
14.] a man was blackmailed "by decoying him into a compromising situation with a prostitute and then confronting him with a confederate who pose[d] as her husband" (Spencer).
16. *still*] forever.   19. *want'st*] lack.
19. *tale*] reckoning.   20. *serve his turn*] suffice for his needs.

PILIA-BORZA.

　No, sir; and therefore I must have five hundred more.

BARABAS.

　I'll rather—

PILIA-BORZA.

　O, good words, sir, and send it you were best; see, there's his
　letter.   25

BARABAS.

　Might he not as well come as send? Pray bid him come and
　fetch it; what he writes for you, ye shall have straight.

PILIA-BORZA.

　Ay, and the rest too, or else—

BARABAS [aside].

　I must make this villain away. [to him] Please you dine with
　me, sir; (aside) and you shall be most heartily poison'd.   30

PILIA-BORZA.

　No, God-a-mercy; shall I have these crowns?

BARABAS.

　I cannot do it; I have lost my keys.

PILIA-BORZA.

　O, if that be all, I can pick ope your locks.

BARABAS.

　Or climb up to my countinghouse window: you know my
　meaning.   35

PILIA-BORZA.

　I know enough, and therefore talk not to me of your
　countinghouse. The gold! or know, Jew, it is in my power
　to hang thee.

BARABAS [aside].

　I am betray'd.
　[to him] 'Tis not five hundred crowns that I esteem,   40
　I am not mov'd at that: this angers me,
　That he who knows I love him as myself
　Should write in this imperious vein! Why, sir,
　You know I have no child, and unto whom

30. aside] Dyce 1; at right-hand
margin after l. 30 Q.

---

29. make this villain away] put this villain to death.
41. mov'd] angered.

Should I leave all but unto Ithamore?   45
PILIA-BORZA.

Here's many words, but no crowns; the crowns!
BARABAS.

Commend me to him, sir, most humbly,
And unto your good mistress, as unknown.
PILIA-BORZA.

Speak, shall I have 'em, sir?
BARABAS.   Sir, here they are.
[aside] O, that I should part with so much gold!   50
[to him] Here, take 'em, fellow, with as good a will—
[aside] As I would see thee hang'd; [to him] O, love stops
    my breath.
Never lov'd man servant as I do Ithamore.
PILIA-BORZA.

I know it, sir.
BARABAS.

Pray when, sir, shall I see you at my house?   55
PILIA-BORZA.

Soon enough to your cost, sir. Fare you well.   Exit.
BARABAS.

Nay, to thine own cost, villain, if thou com'st.
Was ever Jew tormented as I am?
To have a shag-rag knave to come—
Three hundred crowns, and then five hundred crowns!   60
Well, I must seek a means to rid 'em all,
And presently: for in his villainy
He will tell all he knows, and I shall die for 't.
I have it:
I will in some disguise go see the slave,   65
And how the villain revels with my gold.   Exit.

[IV.iv]   Enter Bellamira, Ithamore, [and] Pilia-Borza.

BELLAMIRA.

I'll pledge thee, love, and therefore drink it off.

---

48. as unknown] "i.e., as yet unknown to me" (Bennett).
59. shag-rag] ragged; rascally.
62. presently] immediately.

ITHAMORE.

Say'st thou me so? Have at it! And do you hear?   [*Whispers.*]

BELLAMIRA.

Go to, it shall be so.

ITHAMORE.

Of that condition I will drink it up.

Here's to thee.

BELLAMIRA.   Nay, I'll have all or none.   5

ITHAMORE.

There; if thou lov'st me do not leave a drop.

BELLAMIRA.

Love thee! fill me three glasses.

ITHAMORE.

Three and fifty dozen I'll pledge thee.

PILIA-BORZA.

Knavely spoke, and like a knight at arms.

ITHAMORE.

Hey, *Rivo Castiliano!* a man's a man.   10

BELLAMIRA.

Now to the Jew.

ITHAMORE.

Ha! to the Jew. And send me money you were best!

PILIA-BORZA.

What wouldst thou do if he should send thee none?

ITHAMORE.

Do nothing; but I know what I know. He's a murderer.

BELLAMIRA.

I had not thought he had been so brave a man.   15

ITHAMORE.

You knew Mathias and the governor's son? He and I kill'd
'em both, and yet never touch'd 'em.

5. S.P. BELLAMIRA] *Dyce 1; assigned
to Pil. Q.*

---

2. *me*] to me.   4. *Of*] on.

9. *Knavely*] like a knave; Pilia-Borza plays on the frequent opposition of
knave and *knight*.

10. *Rivo Castiliano!*] a toast of uncertain meaning, perhaps something
akin to "pour down the wine."

PILIA-BORZA.

O, bravely done.

ITHAMORE.

I carried the broth that poison'd the nuns, and he and I,
snicle hand too fast, strangled a friar.   20

BELLAMIRA.

You two alone?

ITHAMORE.

We two; and 'twas never known, nor never shall be for me.

PILIA-BORZA [aside to Bellamira].

This shall with me unto the governor.

BELLAMIRA [aside to Pilia-Borza].

And fit it should; but first let's ha' more gold.—
Come, gentle Ithamore, lie in my lap.   25

ITHAMORE.

Love me little, love me long. Let music rumble,
Whilst I in thy incony lap do tumble.

Enter Barabas *with a lute, disguis'd.*

BELLAMIRA.

A French musician! Come, let's hear your skill.

BARABAS.

Must tuna my lute for sound, twang, twang, first.

ITHAMORE.

Wilt drink, Frenchman? Here's to thee with a—pox on this   30
drunken hiccup!

BARABAS.

Gramercy, monsieur.

BELLAMIRA.

Prithee, Pilia-Borza, bid the fiddler give me the posy in his
hat there.

27. incony] *Reed;* incoomy *Q.*

---

20. *snicle hand too fast*] not satisfactorily explained; *snicle* means "snare,
catch in a noose." Brooke suggests "too free with our noose hand."

22. *for me*] so far as I am concerned.

25. *lie in my lap*] with a sexual suggestion, as in *Hamlet,* III.ii.110.

27. *incony*] pretty, "sexually attractive" (Kirschbaum).

30. *pox*] syphilis—commonly used thus in imprecations and exclamations
of irritation.

32. *Gramercy*] thanks.   33. *posy*] bouquet.

PILIA-BORZA.

Sirrah, you must give my mistress your posy.   35

BARABAS.

A votre commandement, madame.

BELLAMIRA.

How sweet, my Ithamore, the flowers smell.

ITHAMORE.

Like thy breath, sweetheart; no violet like 'em.

PILIA-BORZA.

Foh! methinks they stink like a hollyhock.

BARABAS [aside].

So, now I am reveng'd upon 'em all.   40
The scent thereof was death; I poison'd it.

ITHAMORE.

Play, fiddler, or I'll cut your cat's guts into chitterlings.

BARABAS.

Pardona moy; be no in tune yet. So, now, now all be in.

ITHAMORE.

Give him a crown, and fill me out more wine.

PILIA-BORZA.

There's two crowns for thee; play.   45

BARABAS (aside).

How liberally the villain gives me mine own gold.

PILIA-BORZA.

Methinks he fingers very well.

BARABAS (aside).

So did you when you stole my gold.

PILIA-BORZA.

How swift he runs!

36.] Shone; A voustre commandemente
Madam Q.

_____

36.] at your command, madam.
39. *stink like a hollyhock*] the hollyhock does not have an offensive smell.
42. *cat's guts*] i.e., the strings of the lute.
42. *chitterlings*] smaller intestines of pigs, especially as prepared for eating.
43. *Pardona moy*] Barabas' attempt at *pardonnez moi*, "I beg your pardon."
44. *fill me out*] pour out for me.
47. *fingers*] plays the lute with his fingers; in the next line, Barabas puns
on the meaning "pilfers, filches."
49. *runs*] performs a run on the lute.

BARABAS (*aside*).

You run swifter when you threw my gold out of my window.   50

BELLAMIRA.

Musician, hast been in Malta long?

BARABAS.

Two, three, four month, madam.

ITHAMORE.

Dost not know a Jew, one Barabas?

BARABAS.

Very mush; monsieur, you no be his man?

PILIA-BORZA.

His man!   55

ITHAMORE.

I scorn the peasant; tell him so.

BARABAS [*aside*].

He knows it already.

ITHAMORE.

'Tis a strange thing of that Jew, he lives upon pickled grass-
hoppers, and sauc'd mushrooms.

BARABAS (*aside*).

What a slave's this! The governor feeds not as I do.   60

ITHAMORE.

He never put on clean shirt since he was circumcis'd.

BARABAS (*aside*).

O, rascal! I change myself twice a day.

ITHAMORE.

The hat he wears, Judas left under the elder when he
hang'd himself.

BARABAS (*aside*).

'Twas sent me for a present from the Great Cham.   65

50. *aside*] *Dyce 1; at right-hand*   Q.
margin after l. 50 Q.   60. *aside*] *Dyce 1, at right-hand*
59. mushrooms] *Reed;* Mushrumbs   *margin after l. 60 Q.*

54. *man*] manservant.   59. *sauc'd*] seasoned.
63–64. *Judas...himself*] see Matthew 27 : 5; traditionally the tree Judas
hanged himself on was an elder.
65. *Great Cham*] emperor (or Khan) of the Moguls, of legendary wealth
and power.

PILIA-BORZA.

A masty slave he is. Whither now, fiddler?

BARABAS.

Pardona moy, monsieur, me be no well.   *Exit.*

PILIA-BORZA.

Farewell, fiddler. One letter more to the Jew.

BELLAMIRA.

Prithee, sweet love, one more, and write it sharp.

ITHAMORE.

No, I'll send by word of mouth now. Bid him deliver thee a   70
thousand crowns, by the same token that the nuns lov'd
rice, that Friar Barnardine slept in his own clothes—any of
'em will do it.

PILIA-BORZA.

Let me alone to urge it, now I know the meaning.

ITHAMORE.

The meaning has a meaning. Come, let's in;   75
To undo a Jew is charity, and not sin.   *Exeunt.*

[V.i]
        Enter Ferneze, Knights, Martin del Bosco [, *and Officers*].

FERNEZE.

Now, gentlemen, betake you to your arms,
And see that Malta be well fortified;
And it behooves you to be resolute,
For Calymath, having hover'd here so long,
Will win the town, or die before the walls.   5

I KNIGHT.

And die he shall, for we will never yield.

        Enter Bellamira [*and*] Pilia-Borza.

BELLAMIRA.

O, bring us to the governor!

67. me] *Reed;* we *Q*.

---

66. *masty*] (1) fattened, as used of a swine; or (2) burly, big-bodied.
69. *sharp*] sharply, peremptorily.
75. *The meaning has a meaning*] ? the meaning brings lamentation (for
Barabas).
[V.i]
4. *hover'd*] hesitated before taking action.

FERNEZE.

Away with her, she is a courtesan.

BELLAMIRA.

Whate'er I am, yet, governor, hear me speak.
I bring thee news by whom thy son was slain: 10
Mathias did it not, it was the Jew.

PILIA-BORZA.

Who, besides the slaughter of these gentlemen,
Poison'd his own daughter and the nuns,
Strangled a friar, and I know not what
Mischief beside.

FERNEZE.   Had we but proof of this—   15

BELLAMIRA.

Strong proof, my lord. His man's now at my lodging
That was his agent; he'll confess it all.

FERNEZE.

Go fetch him straight. [*Exeunt Officers.*] I always fear'd that
Jew.

Enter [Officers with] Barabas [and] Ithamore.

BARABAS.

I'll go alone; dogs, do not hale me thus.

ITHAMORE.

Nor me neither. I cannot outrun you, constable. O, my   20
belly!

BARABAS [*aside*].

One dram of powder more had made all sure.
What a damn'd slave was I!

FERNEZE.

Make fires, heat irons, let the rack be fetch'd.

I KNIGHT.

Nay, stay, my lord; 't may be he will confess.   25

BARABAS.

Confess! What mean you, lords? Who should confess?

FERNEZE.

Thou and thy Turk; 'twas you that slew my son.

---

15. *Mischief*] wickedness.
19. *hale*] drag.
23. *damn'd slave*] i.e., "stupid idiot."
24. *rack*] a device for torture by stretching the body.

ITHAMORE.

Guilty, my lord, I confess. Your son and Mathias were
both contracted unto Abigail. He forg'd a counterfeit challenge.   30

BARABAS.

Who carried that challenge?

ITHAMORE.

I carried it, I confess, but who writ it? Marry, even he that
strangled Barnardine, poison'd the nuns, and his own
daughter.

FERNEZE.

Away with him! His sight is death to me.   35

BARABAS.

For what? You men of Malta, hear me speak.
She is a courtesan, and he a thief,
And he my bondman. Let me have law,
For none of this can prejudice my life.

FERNEZE.

Once more, away with him! You shall have law.   40

BARABAS.

Devils, do your worst! I live in spite of you!
As these have spoke, so be it to their souls.
[aside] I hope the poison'd flowers will work anon.
[Exeunt Officers with Barabas, Ithamore, Pilia-Borza, and Bellamira.]

Enter Katherine.

KATHERINE.

Was my Mathias murder'd by the Jew?
Ferneze, 'twas thy son that murder'd him.   45

FERNEZE.

Be patient, gentle madam; it was he.
He forged the daring challenge made them fight.

KATHERINE.

Where is the Jew? Where is that murderer?

FERNEZE.

In prison till the law has pass'd on him.

29. He] *Reed; not in* Q.   43.1.] *Scott* (subs.); *Exit.* Q.

32. *Marry*] why, to be sure.   37. *he*] Pilia-Borza.
38. *he*] Ithamore.   38. *bondman*] slave.
39. *prejudice*] be prejudicial to.   43. *anon*] at once.

Enter Officer.

1 OFFICER.

    My lord, the courtesan and her man are dead;   50
    So is the Turk, and Barabas the Jew.

FERNEZE.

    Dead?

1 OFFICER.

    Dead, my lord, and here they bring his body.

        [*Enter Officers, carrying* Barabas *as dead.*]

DEL BOSCO.

    This sudden death of his is very strange.

FERNEZE.

    Wonder not at it, sir, the heavens are just: 55
    Their deaths were like their lives; then think not of 'em.
    Since they are dead, let them be buried.
    For the Jew's body, throw that o'er the walls,
    To be a prey for vultures and wild beasts.
    So, now away, and fortify the town.   60
        Exeunt. [*Manet* Barabas.]

BARABAS.

    What, all alone? well fare, sleepy drink.
    I'll be reveng'd on this accursed town,
    For by my means Calymath shall enter in.
    I'll help to slay their children and their wives,
    To fire the churches, pull their houses down.   65
    Take my goods, too, and seize upon my lands;
    I hope to see the governor a slave,
    And, rowing in a galley, whipp'd to death.

        Enter Calymath, *Bashaws,* [*and*] *Turks.*

CALYMATH.

    Whom have we there, a spy?

BARABAS.

    Yes, my good lord, one that can spy a place   70
    Where you may enter, and surprise the town.

---

    61. *well fare*] farewell.   61. *sleepy*] sleep-inducing.
    70. *spy*] discover.
    71. *surprise the town*] capture the town suddenly.

My name is Barabas; I am a Jew.

CALYMATH.

Art thou that Jew whose goods we heard were sold
For tribute money?

BARABAS.   The very same, my lord.

And since that time they have hir'd a slave, my man,   75
To accuse me of a thousand villainies.
I was imprison'd, but escap'd their hands.

CALYMATH.

Didst break prison?

BARABAS.

No, no:
I drank of poppy and cold mandrake juice,   80
And, being asleep, belike they thought me dead,
And threw me o'er the walls; so, or how else,
The Jew is here, and rests at your command.

CALYMATH.

'Twas bravely done. But tell me, Barabas,
Canst thou, as thou report'st, make Malta ours?   85

BARABAS.

Fear not, my lord, for here, against the truce,
The rock is hollow, and of purpose digg'd,
To make a passage for the running streams
And common channels of the city.
Now whilst you give assault unto the walls,   90
I'll lead five hundred soldiers through the vault,
And rise with them i' th' middle of the town,
Open the gates for you to enter in,
And by this means the city is your own.

CALYMATH.

If this be true, I'll make thee governor.   95

BARABAS.

And if it be not true, then let me die.

---

77. escap'd] *Scott;* scap'd *Q*.   85. report'st] *Reed;* reportest *Q*.

---

80. *poppy . . . mandrake*] opium, mandragora, plants with narcotic effect.
86. *against the truce*] either (1) contrary to the treaty or (2) in anticipation
of the cessation of hostilities.
89. *common channels*] public gutters.
91. *vault*] sewer.

CALYMATH.

Thou'st doom'd thyself. Assault it presently.   *Exeunt.*

[V.ii]

Alarms. Enter Turks [*and*] Barabas [*with*] Ferneze and *Knights prisoners.*

CALYMATH.

Now vail your pride, you captive Christians,
And kneel for mercy to your conquering foe.
Now where's the hope you had of haughty Spain?
Ferneze, speak: had it not been much better
To 've kept thy promise than be thus surpris'd?   5

FERNEZE.

What should I say? We are captives and must yield.

CALYMATH.

Ay, villains, you must yield; and under Turkish yokes
Shall groaning bear the burden of our ire.
And, Barabas, as erst we promis'd thee,
For thy desert we make thee governor;   10
Use them at thy discretion.

BARABAS.   Thanks, my lord.

FERNEZE.

O, fatal day, to fall into the hands
Of such a traitor and unhallowed Jew!
What greater misery could heaven inflict?

CALYMATH.

'Tis our command; and, Barabas, we give   15
To guard thy person, these our Janizaries:
Entreat them well, as we have used thee.
And now, brave bashaws, come, we'll walk about
The ruin'd town, and see the wrack we made.
Farewell, brave Jew; farewell, great Barabas.   20

Exeunt [Calymath *and Bashaws*].

5. To 've] *Cunningham;* To *Q.*

---

97. *presently*] immediately.
[V.ii]
0.1. *Alarms*] sounds of battle (offstage).   1. *vail*] humble.
5. *surpris'd*] captured without warning.   9. *erst*] not long ago.
16. *Janizaries*] members of a body of Turkish infantry, constituting the
main part of the army.
17. *Entreat*] treat.   19. *wrack*] destruction.

BARABAS.

    May all good fortune follow Calymath.

    And now, as entrance to our safety,

    To prison with the governor and these

    Captains, his consorts and confederates.

FERNEZE.

    O, villain, heaven will be reveng'd on thee!   25

BARABAS.

    Away! no more! let him not trouble me.

                      Exeunt. [*Manet* Barabas.]

    Thus hast thou gotten, by thy policy,

    No simple place, no small authority.

    I now am governor of Malta. True,

    But Malta hates me, and in hating me   30

    My life's in danger, and what boots it thee,

    Poor Barabas, to be the governor,

    Whenas thy life shall be at their command?

    No, Barabas, this must be look'd into;

    And since by wrong thou gott'st authority,   35

    Maintain it bravely by firm policy;

    At least unprofitably lose it not.

    For he that liveth in authority,

    And neither gets him friends nor fills his bags,

    Lives like the ass that Aesop speaketh of,   40

    That labors with a load of bread and wine,

    And leaves it off to snap on thistle tops.

    But Barabas will be more circumspect.

    Begin betimes. Occasion's bald behind;

    Slip not thine opportunity, for fear too late   45

26.1. *Exeunt*] Penley; *under* thee
(*l. 25*) Q.

---

22. *entrance*] beginning.   24. *consorts*] colleagues in authority.

28. *simple place*] insignificant position.   31. *boots*] avails.

33. *Whenas*] inasmuch as.   33. *at their command*] under their control.

34. *look'd into*] examined minutely.

37. *unprofitably*] without advantage.

39. *fills his bags*] i.e., with gold.   42. *leaves it off*] abstains from it.

42. *snap*] feed in quick bites.   44. *betimes*] soon; before it is too late.

44. *Occasion's bald behind*] i.e., Opportunity (personified as a female) must be seized ("taken by the forelock") before it passes one by.

45. *Slip not*] don't fail to take advantage of.

Thou seek'st for much, but canst not compass it.
Within here!

Enter Ferneze *with a Guard.*

FERNEZE.

My lord?

BARABAS.

Ay, "lord"; thus slaves will learn.
Now, governor—stand by there; wait within—   50

[*Exeunt Guard.*]

This is the reason that I sent for thee:
Thou seest thy life, and Malta's happiness,
Are at my arbitrament, and Barabas
At his discretion may dispose of both.
Now tell me, governor, and plainly too,   55
What think'st thou shall become of it and thee?

FERNEZE.

This, Barabas: since things are in thy power,
I see no reason but of Malta's wrack,
Nor hope of thee but extreme cruelty;
Nor fear I death, nor will I flatter thee.   60

BARABAS.

Governor, good words; be not so furious.
'Tis not thy life which can avail me aught;
Yet you do live, and live for me you shall.
And as for Malta's ruin, think you not
'Twere slender policy for Barabas   65
To dispossess himself of such a place?
For sith, as once you said, within this isle,
In Malta here, that I have got my goods,
And in this city still have had success,
And now at length am grown your governor,   70
Yourselves shall see it shall not be forgot:
For as a friend not known but in distress,

---

53. *at my arbitrament*] in my absolute power.
54. *dispose of*] do what he wishes with.
61. *good words*] used elliptically for "do not speak so fiercely" (*OED*).
63. *Yet*] still.   63. *for me*] so far as I am concerned.
65. *slender*] weak, flimsy.   67. *sith*] since.
69. *still*] now as before.

I'll rear up Malta, now remediless.

FERNEZE.

Will Barabas recover Malta's loss?
Will Barabas be good to Christians?   75

BARABAS.

What wilt thou give me, governor, to procure
A dissolution of the slavish bands
Wherein the Turk hath yok'd your land and you?
What will you give me if I render you
The life of Calymath, surprise his men,   80
And in an outhouse of the city shut
His soldiers, till I have consum'd 'em all with fire?
What will you give him that procureth this?

FERNEZE.

Do but bring this to pass which thou pretendest,
Deal truly with us as thou intimatest,   85
And I will send amongst the citizens
And by my letters privately procure
Great sums of money for thy recompense:
Nay, more, do this, and live thou governor still.

BARABAS.

Nay, do thou this, Ferneze, and be free.   90
Governor, I enlarge thee; live with me,
Go walk about the city, see thy friends.
Tush, send not letters to 'em, go thyself,
And let me see what money thou canst make.
Here is my hand that I'll set Malta free,   95
And thus we cast it: to a solemn feast
I will invite young Selim Calymath,
Where be thou present only to perform
One stratagem that I'll impart to thee,
Wherein no danger shall betide thy life,   100

---

73. *rear up*] raise, exalt.   73. *remediless*] having no prospect of rescue.
77. *bands*] chains.   79. *render*] deliver up to.
80. *surprise*] suddenly capture.
81. *outhouse of*] building adjoining (in this instance a monastery; see V.iii. 36–37).
84. *pretendest*] (1) claim to have the power to do (2) plan.
87. *privately*] secretly.   91. *enlarge thee*] release thee from confinement.
96. *cast*] contrive.   100. *betide*] happen to.

And I will warrant Malta free for ever.
FERNEZE.
    Here is my hand. Believe me, Barabas,
    I will be there, and do as thou desirest.
    When is the time?
BARABAS.   Governor, presently.
    For Calymath, when he hath view'd the town,   105
    Will take his leave and sail toward Ottoman.
FERNEZE.
    Then will I, Barabas, about this coin,
    And bring it with me to thee in the evening.
BARABAS.
    Do so, but fail not; now farewell, Ferneze.   [*Exit* Ferneze.]
    And thus far roundly goes the business.   110
    Thus, loving neither, will I live with both,
    Making a profit of my policy;
    And he from whom my most advantage comes
    Shall be my friend.
    This is the life we Jews are us'd to lead;   115
    And reason, too, for Christians do the like.
    Well, now about effecting this device.
    First to surprise great Selim's soldiers,
    And then to make provision for the feast,
    That at one instant all things may be done.   120
    My policy detests prevention.
    To what event my secret purpose drives,
    I know; and they shall witness with their lives.   *Exit.*

[V.iii]   *Enter* Calymath [*and*] *Bashaws.*

CALYMATH.
    Thus have we view'd the city, seen the sack,

---

    104. *presently*] immediately.   106. *Ottoman*] Turkey.
    107.] i.e., I'll get busy raising the money.
    110. *roundly*] "successfully, in a thorough-going manner" (Bennett).
    115. *us'd*] accustomed.   116. *And reason*] and with reason.
    121. *prevention*] "action of...stopping another person in the execution
of his design" (*OED*).
    122. *event*] outcome.
[V.iii]
    1. *sack*] results of plundering.

And caus'd the ruins to be new repair'd,
Which with our bombards' shot and basilisk
We rent in sunder at our entry.
And now I see the situation,   5
And how secure this conquer'd island stands,
Environ'd with the Mediterranean Sea,
Strong countermur'd with other petty isles,
And toward Calabria, back'd by Sicily
(Where Syracusian Dionysius reign'd),   10
Two lofty turrets that command the town,
I wonder how it could be conquer'd thus.

Enter a Messenger.

MESSENGER.

From Barabas, Malta's governor, I bring
A message unto mighty Calymath:
Hearing his Sovereign was bound for sea,   15
To sail to Turkey, to great Ottoman,
He humbly would entreat your Majesty
To come and see his homely citadel,
And banquet with him ere thou leav'st the isle.

CALYMATH.

To banquet with him in his citadel?   20
I fear me, messenger, to feast my train
Within a town of war so lately pillag'd
Will be too costly and too troublesome.
Yet would I gladly visit Barabas,
For well has Barabas deserv'd of us.   25

MESSENGER.

Selim, for that, thus saith the governor,
That he hath in store a pearl so big,

8. countermur'd] *conj. Deighton;*   10–11.] *transposed by Robinson.*
contermin'd Q.   10. Where] *Robinson;* When Q.

3. *bombards*] cannons (the earliest kind).
3. *basilisk*] large brass cannon.   9. *Calabria*] a region in Italy.
10. *Syracusian Dionysius*] the elder or younger Dionysius, tyrants (rulers)
of Syracuse, in Sicily, in the fourth century B.C.
16. *Ottoman*] the sultan of Turkey.
21. *train*] retinue.   27. *in store*] in reserve.

So precious, and withal so orient,
As, be it valued but indifferently,
The price thereof will serve to entertain   30
Selim and all his soldiers for a month;
Therefore he humbly would entreat your Highness
Not to depart till he has feasted you.

CALYMATH.

I cannot feast my men in Malta walls,
Except he place his tables in the streets.   35

MESSENGER.

Know, Selim, that there is a monastery
Which standeth as an outhouse to the town;
There will he banquet them, but thee at home,
With all thy bashaws and brave followers.

CALYMATH.

Well, tell the governor we grant his suit;   40
We'll in this summer evening feast with him.

MESSENGER.

I shall, my lord.   *Exit.*

CALYMATH.

And now, bold bashaws, let us to our tents,
And meditate how we may grace us best
To solemnize our governor's great feast.   *Exeunt.*   45

[V.iv]   *Enter* Ferneze, Knights, [*and* Martin] del Bosco.

FERNEZE.

In this, my countrymen, be rul'd by me.
Have special care that no man sally forth
Till you shall hear a culverin discharg'd
By him that bears the linstock, kindled thus;
Then issue out and come to rescue me,   5
For happily I shall be in distress,

---

28. *orient*] lustrous.   29. *indifferently*] impartially.
35. *Except*] unless.   44. *meditate*] consider.
44. *grace us*] adorn ourselves.   45. *solemnize*] dignify by ceremonies.
[V.iv]
    3. *culverin*] cannon ("very long in proportion to its bore" [*OED*]).
    4. *linstock*] a staff for holding the match to ignite the charge.
    6. *happily*] perchance.

Or you released of this servitude.

I KNIGHT.

Rather than thus to live as Turkish thralls,
What will we not adventure?

FERNEZE.

On then, be gone.

KNIGHTS.   Farewell, grave governor.   [*Exeunt.*]   10

[V.v]

Enter [Barabas] *with a hammer above, very busy* [*, and* Carpenters].

BARABAS.

How stand the cords? How hang these hinges? Fast?
Are all the cranes and pulleys sure?

I CARPENTER.   All fast.

BARABAS.

Leave nothing loose, all level'd to my mind.
Why, now I see that you have art indeed.
There, carpenters, divide that gold amongst you.   5
Go swill in bowls of sack and muscadine:
Down to the cellar; taste of all my wines.

CARPENTERS.

We shall, my lord, and thank you.   *Exeunt.*

BARABAS.

And if you like them, drink your fill and die;
For so I live, perish may all the world.   10
Now, Selim Calymath, return me word
That thou wilt come, and I am satisfied.

Enter Messenger.

Now, sirrah, what, will he come?

[V.v]	8. S.P. CARPENTERS] *Reed; Carp. Q.*
2. S.P. I CARPENTER] *Dyce 1; Serv.*	12.1. *Enter* Messenger] *Dyce 1;*
Q.	*after l. 13 Q.*

8. *thralls*] slaves, captives.
[V.v]
0.1. *above*] i.e., on the upper stage.
3. *level'd to my mind*] directed according to my wishes.
4. *art*] skill.   6. *sack*] a white wine.
6. *muscadine*] muscatel, a strong sweet wine.
9.] "Barabas has poisoned the wine to remove the witnesses of his crimes" (Bennett).

MESSENGER.

He will; and has commanded all his men
To come ashore, and march through Malta streets, 15
That thou mayst feast them in thy citadel.

BARABAS.

Then now are all things as my wish would have 'em.
There wanteth nothing but the governor's pelf,

Enter Ferneze.

And see, he brings it. Now, governor, the sum?

FERNEZE.

With free consent, a hundred thousand pounds. 20

BARABAS.

Pounds, say'st thou, governor? Well, since it is no more,
I'll satisfy myself with that. Nay, keep it still,
For if I keep not promise, trust not me.
And, governor, now partake my policy:
First, for his army, they are sent before, 25
Enter'd the monastery, and underneath
In several places are fieldpieces pitch'd,
Bombards, whole barrels full of gunpowder,
That on the sudden shall dissever it,
And batter all the stones about their ears, 30
Whence none can possibly escape alive.
Now as for Calymath and his consorts,
Here have I made a dainty gallery,
The floor whereof, this cable being cut,
Doth fall asunder, so that it doth sink 35
Into a deep pit past recovery.
Here, hold that knife, and when thou seest he comes,
And with his bashaws shall be blithely set,
A warning-piece shall be shot off from the tower,
To give thee knowledge when to cut the cord, 40

18.1. *Enter* Ferneze] *after l. 19 Q.*

---

18. *pelf*] money.   22. *still*] for now.
24. *partake*] be made acquainted with.   25. *before*] ahead.
27. *fieldpieces pitch'd*] light cannon set up.
29. *dissever it*] break the monastery in pieces.
33. *dainty*] delightful.   38. *blithely set*] seated in a merry mood.
39. *warning-piece*] signal gun.

And fire the house. Say, will not this be brave?

FERNEZE.

O, excellent! Here, hold thee, Barabas,
I trust thy word; take what I promis'd thee.

BARABAS.

No, governor, I'll satisfy thee first;
Thou shalt not live in doubt of anything.   45
Stand close, for here they come. [Ferneze *retires*.] Why, is
   not this
A kingly kind of trade, to purchase towns
By treachery, and sell 'em by deceit?
Now tell me, worldlings, underneath the sun,
If greater falsehood ever has been done?   50

Enter Calymath *and* Bashaws.

CALYMATH.

Come, my companion bashaws, see, I pray,
How busy Barabas is there above
To entertain us in his gallery.
Let us salute him. Save thee, Barabas.

BARABAS.

Welcome, great Calymath.   55

FERNEZE [*aside*].

How the slave jeers at him!

BARABAS.

Will 't please thee, mighty Selim Calymath,
To ascend our homely stairs?

CALYMATH.   Ay, Barabas.

Come, bashaws, attend.

FERNEZE.   Stay, Calymath!

For I will show thee greater courtesy   60
Than Barabas would have afforded thee.

---

49. sun] *Reed;* summe *Q*.

---

42. *hold thee*] take it.
46. *close*] concealed.
49. *worldlings*] i.e., "you in the audience who are devoted to material
things."
54. *salute*] greet.
54. *Save thee*] short for "God save thee," a greeting.

1 KNIGHT [*within*].
    Sound a charge there!

A charge [sounded within;] the cable cut [by Ferneze; the floor of the upper stage giving way, Barabas falls into] a caldron, discovered [below].

[*Enter Martin del Bosco and Knights.*]

CALYMATH.
    How now! what means this?
BARABAS.
    Help, help me! Christians, help!
FERNEZE.
    See, Calymath, this was devis'd for thee.   65
CALYMATH.
    Treason, treason! Bashaws, fly!
FERNEZE.
    No, Selim, do not fly.
    See his end first, and fly then if thou canst.
BARABAS.
    O, help me, Selim; help me, Christians.
    Governor, why stand you all so pitiless?   70
FERNEZE.
    Should I in pity of thy plaints or thee,
    Accursed Barabas, base Jew, relent?
    No, thus I'll see thy treachery repaid,
    But wish thou hadst behav'd thee otherwise.
BARABAS.
    You will not help me, then?
FERNEZE.   No, villain, no.   75
BARABAS.
    And, villains, know you cannot help me now.
    Then, Barabas, breathe forth thy latest fate,
    And in the fury of thy torments, strive
    To end thy life with resolution.
    Know, governor, 'twas I that slew thy son;   80
    I fram'd the challenge that did make them meet.

---

62. *charge*] trumpet call.   62.2. *discovered*] revealed.
71. *plaints*] lamentations.   77. *latest*] last.
79. *resolution*] unyielding temper.   81. *fram'd*] devised, composed.

Know, Calymath, I aim'd thy overthrow,
And had I but escap'd this stratagem,
I would have brought confusion on you all,
Damn'd Christians, dogs, and Turkish infidels.   85
But now begins the extremity of heat
To pinch me with intolerable pangs:
Die, life! fly, soul! tongue, curse thy fill and die!   [*Dies.*]

CALYMATH.
Tell me, you Christians, what doth this portend?

FERNEZE.
This train he laid to have entrapp'd thy life.   90
Now, Selim, note the unhallowed deeds of Jews;
Thus he determin'd to have handled thee,
But I have rather chose to save thy life.

CALYMATH.
Was this the banquet he prepar'd for us?
Let's hence, lest further mischief be pretended.   95

FERNEZE.
Nay, Selim, stay, for since we have thee here,
We will not let thee part so suddenly:
Besides, if we should let thee go, all's one,
For with thy galleys couldst thou not get hence,
Without fresh men to rig and furnish them.   100

CALYMATH.
Tush, governor, take thou no care for that;
My men are all aboard,
And do attend my coming there by this.

FERNEZE.
Why, heard'st thou not the trumpet sound a charge?

CALYMATH.
Yes, what of that?

FERNEZE.   Why then the house was fir'd,   105

---

82. *aim'd*] planned.   84. *confusion*] destruction.
86. *extremity*] extreme intensity.   87. *pinch*] torment.
90. *train he laid*] trick he devised.   95. *mischief*] evil.
95. *pretended*] intended, planned.
98. *all's one*] "it wouldn't make any difference."
100. *fresh*] different.   100. *furnish*] (1) fit out (2) garrison.
101. *take thou no care for that*] "don't worry about that."
103. *attend*] wait for.   103. *by this*] by this time.

Blown up, and all thy soldiers massacred.

CALYMATH.

O, monstrous treason!

FERNEZE.   A Jew's courtesy;
For he that did by treason work our fall,
By treason hath delivered thee to us.
Know, therefore, till thy father hath made good   110
The ruins done to Malta and to us,
Thou canst not part; for Malta shall be freed,
Or Selim ne'er return to Ottoman.

CALYMATH.

Nay, rather, Christians, let me go to Turkey,
In person there to meditate your peace;   115
To keep me here will naught advantage you.

FERNEZE.

Content thee, Calymath; here thou must stay,
And live in Malta prisoner; for come all the world
To rescue thee, so will we guard us now,
As sooner shall they drink the ocean dry   120
Than conquer Malta, or endanger us.
So march away, and let due praise be given
Neither to fate nor fortune, but to heaven.   [*Exeunt.*]

Finis.

118. all] *Reed;* ·call *Q*.

108. *work*] bring about.
115. *meditate*] plan (by revolving in the mind).
116. *naught advantage you*] benefit you in no way.

Epilogue Spoken at Court

It is our fear, dread Sovereign, we have been
Too tedious; neither can 't be less than sin
To wrong your princely patience: if we have,
Thus low dejected, we your pardon crave;
And if aught here offend your ear or sight,   5
We only act, and speak, what others write.

0.1.] *epilogue appears on A4 beneath*   0.1. Spoken at Court] *from the*
The Prologue spoken at Court. *Q.*   *heading to the prologue in Q.*

1. *dread*] held in awe, revered.
4. *low dejected*] i.e., the actors are bowing.

Epilogue to the Stage

In graving, with Pygmalion to contend,
Or painting, with Apelles, doubtless the end
Must be disgrace; our actor did not so:
He only aim'd to go, but not outgo.
Nor think that this day any prize was play'd;   5
Here were no bets at all, no wagers laid;
All the ambition that his mind doth swell
Is but to hear from you (by me) 'twas well.

0.1.] *epilogue appears on A4v beneath*   0.1. to the Stage] *from the heading to*
The Prologue to the Stage, at the   *the prologue in Q.*
Cocke-pit. *Q.*

---

1. *graving*] sculpturing.
1. *Pygmalion*] legendary king of Cyprus who made a statue so beautiful
he fell in love with it; Aphrodite brought the statue to life. Hence Pygmalion is the type of the consummate artist.
2. *Apelles*] "the greatest painter of antiquity" (Harvey).
4. *go*] have a certain degree of excellence.
4. *outgo*] surpass.
5. *prize was play'd*] contest was engaged in.
6. *no wagers laid*] apparently it was not uncommon to make wagers "as to the comparative merits of rival actors" (Bennett).

Appendix

Chronology

Approximate years are indicated by *, occurrences in doubt by (?).

Political and Literary Events	Life and Major Works of Marlowe
1558 Accession of Queen Elizabeth. Robert Greene born. Thomas Kyd born.	
1560 George Chapman born.	
1561 Francis Bacon born.	
1564 Shakespeare born.	Christopher Marlowe born at Canterbury; baptized February 26.
1570 Thomas Heywood born.*	
1572 Thomas Dekker born.* John Donne born. Massacre of St. Bartholomew's Day.	
1573 Ben Jonson born.*	
1576 The Theatre, the first permanent public theater in London, established by James Burbage. John Marston born.	
1577 The Curtain theater opened. Holinshed's *Chronicles of England, Scotland and Ireland*.	

Drake begins circumnavigation of the earth; completed 1580.

1579

John Fletcher born.

John Lyly's *Euphues: The Anatomy of Wit* published.

Sir Thomas North's translation of Plutarch's *Lives*.

Enters as scholar at King's School, Canterbury.

1580

Thomas Middleton born.

Enters Corpus Christi College, Cambridge.

1583

Philip Massinger born.

1584

Francis Beaumont born.*

Receives Cambridge B.A.

1585

Engages in secret government service.*

1586

Death of Sir Philip Sidney.

John Ford born.

DIDO, QUEEN OF CARTHAGE (with Nashe).

1587

The Rose theater opened by Henslowe.

Execution of Mary, Queen of Scots.

Drake raids Cadiz.

Receives Cambridge M.A. upon intervention of the Privy Council. *TAMBURLAINE*, Part I.*

1588

Defeat of the Spanish Armada.

TAMBURLAINE, Part II.*

1589

Greene's *FRIAR BACON AND FRIAR BUNGAY.*

Kyd's *THE SPANISH TRAGEDY.*

Imprisoned in Newgate for a street fight.

1590

Spenser's *Faerie Queene* (Books I–III) published.

Sidney's *Arcadia* published.

Shakespeare's *HENRY VI*, Parts I–III,* *TITUS ANDRONICUS.*

THE JEW OF MALTA.

1591

Shakespeare's *RICHARD III.*

1592

Shakespeare's *TAMING OF THE*

Summoned on a charge of assault.

SHREW* and *THE COMEDY OF ERRORS.*
Death of Greene.

In government service at the siege of Rouen (?).
THE MASSACRE AT PARIS, *DOCTOR FAUSTUS,* *EDWARD II.**

1593
Shakespeare's *LOVE'S LABOUR'S LOST;* *Venus and Adonis* published. Theaters closed on account of plague.

Summoned to appear before the Privy Council, May 18, on a charge of heresy.
Killed by Ingram Frizer in a tavern at Deptford, May 30.

1594
Shakespeare's *TWO GENTLEMEN OF VERONA;* *The Rape of Lucrece* published.
Shakespeare's company becomes Lord Chamberlain's Men.
James Shirley born.*
Death of Kyd.

1595
The Swan theater built.
Sidney's *Defense of Poesy* published.
Shakespeare's *ROMEO AND JULIET,* *A MIDSUMMER NIGHT'S DREAM,* *RICHARD II.**
Raleigh's first expedition to Guiana.

All Ovid's Elegies published (translation).*

1596
Spenser's *Faerie Queene* (Books IV–VI) published.
Shakespeare's *MERCHANT OF VENICE,* *KING JOHN.**

1597
Bacon's *Essays* (first edition).
Shakespeare's *HENRY IV*, Part I.*

1598
Demolition of the Theatre.
Shakespeare's *MUCH ADO ABOUT NOTHING,* *HENRY IV*, Part II.*
Jonson's *EVERY MAN IN HIS HUMOR* (first version).
Seven books of Chapman's translation of Homer's *Iliad* published.

Hero and Leander published.

1599

The Globe theater opened.
Shakespeare's *AS YOU LIKE IT*,*
HENRY V,* *JULIUS CAESAR*.*
Dekker's *THE SHOEMAKERS'
HOLIDAY*.*
Death of Spenser.

1600

Shakespeare's *TWELFTH
NIGHT*,* *HAMLET*.* Marston's
ANTONIO AND MELLIDA,*
ANTONIO'S REVENGE.*
The Fortune theater built by
Alleyn.

*Lucan's First Book Translated Line for
Line* published.

1601

Shakespeare's *MERRY WIVES OF
WINDSOR*.*
Insurrection and execution of the
Earl of Essex.

1602

Shakespeare's *TROILUS AND
CRESSIDA*,* *ALL'S WELL THAT
ENDS WELL*.*

1603

Death of Queen Elizabeth; accession of James VI of Scotland as
James I.
Florio's translation of Montaigne's
Essays published.
Heywood's *A WOMAN KILLED
WITH KINDNESS*.
Marston's *THE MALCONTENT*.*
Shakespeare's company becomes
the King's Men.

1604

Shakespeare's *MEASURE FOR
MEASURE*,* *OTHELLO*.*
Marston's *THE FAWN*.*
Chapman's *BUSSY D'AMBOIS*.*

1605

Shakespeare's *KING LEAR*.*

Marston's *THE DUTCH COUR-
TEZAN.*·
Bacon's *Advancement of Learning*
published.
The Gunpowder Plot.

1606
Shakespeare's *MACBETH.*
Jonson's *VOLPONE.*
Tourneur's *REVENGER'S
TRAGEDY.*
The Red Bull theater built.
Death of John Lyly.

1607
Shakespeare's *ANTONY AND
CLEOPATRA.*
Beaumont's *KNIGHT OF THE
BURNING PESTLE.*
Settlement of Jamestown, Virginia.

1608
Shakespeare's *CORIOLANUS,*
TIMON OF ATHENS,* PERI-
CLES.*
Chapman's *CONSPIRACY AND
TRAGEDY OF CHARLES, DUKE
OF BYRON.*
Dekker's *Gull's Hornbook* published.
Richard Burbage leases Blackfriars
Theatre for King's Company.
John Milton born.

1609
Shakespeare's *CYMBELINE;*
Sonnets* published.
Jonson's *EPICOENE.*

1610
Jonson's *ALCHEMIST.*
Chapman's *REVENGE OF BUSSY
D'AMBOIS.*
Richard Crashaw born.

1611
Authorized (King James) Version
of the Bible published.
Shakespeare's *THE WINTER'S*

TALE, THE TEMPEST.*
Beaumont and Fletcher's *A KING
AND NO KING.*
Tourneur's *ATHEIST'S
TRAGEDY.**
Chapman's translation of *Iliad*
completed.

1612
Webster's *THE WHITE DEVIL.**

1613
The Globe theater burned.
Shakespeare's *HENRY VIII* (with
Fletcher).
Webster's *THE DUCHESS OF
MALFI.**
Middleton's *A CHASTE MAID IN
CHEAPSIDE.*
Sir Thomas Overbury murdered.

1614
The Globe theater rebuilt.
The Hope Theatre built.
Jonson's *BARTHOLOMEW FAIR.*

1616
Publication of Folio edition of
Jonson's *Works.*
Death of Shakespeare.
Death of Beaumont.

1618
Outbreak of Thirty Years War.
Execution of Raleigh.

1620
Pilgrim Fathers land at Plymouth.

1621
Middleton's *WOMEN BEWARE
WOMEN.**
Robert Burton's *Anatomy of Melan-
choly* published.
Andrew Marvell born.

1622
Middleton and Rowley's *THE
CHANGELING.**
Henry Vaughan born.

1623
Publication of Folio edition of
Shakespeare's *COMEDIES,
HISTORIES, AND TRAGEDIES.*

1625
Death of King James I; accession of
Charles I.
Death of Fletcher.

1626
Death of Tourneur.
Death of Bacon.

1627
Death of Middleton.

1628
Ford's *THE LOVER'S MELAN-
CHOLY.*
Petition of Right.
Buckingham assassinated.

1631
Shirley's *THE TRAITOR.*
Death of Donne.

1632
Death of Dekker.*

1633
Donne's *Poems* published.
Massinger's *THE CITY MADAM.**
Death of George Herbert.

1634
Death of Chapman, Marston, Webster.*
THE TWO NOBLE KINSMEN
published.

1635
Sir Thomas Browne's *Religio
Medici.*

1637
Death of Jonson.

1639
First Bishops' War.
Death of Carew.*

1640
Short Parliament.
Long Parliament impeaches Laud.
Death of Massinger, Burton.

1641
Irish rebel.
Death of Heywood.

1642
Charles I leaves London; Civil War breaks out.
Shirley's *COURT SECRET*.
All theaters closed by Act of Parliament.

1643
Parliament swears to the Solemn League and Covenant.

1645
Ordinance for New Model Army enacted.

1646
End of First Civil War.

1647
Army occupies London.
Charles I forms alliance with Scots.
Beaumont and Fletcher First Folio published.